Sarah's Laughter

Vinoth Ramachandra's writing is not for the faint of heart or mind – and that is precisely why this book is such a gift. When facing some of life's deepest pain and loss – a personal reality known to Ramachandra himself – you want a guide who is unshirkingly honest and unapologetically rigorous on existential, theological, and spiritual levels. Ramachandra delivers just this and with it offers a powerful recalibration of hope.

Mark Labberton, PhD
President,
Fuller Theological Seminary, Pasadena, California, USA

In *Sarah's Laughter* one of Asia's finest Christian thinkers offers a compellingly articulate and authentically human response to the age-old question of human pain and suffering that goes beyond shallow theodicies and glib answers towards a biblical realism that is both true to reason and true to life. Ramachandra's creative, theological genius is at its best in the robust treatment of relevant biblical material, wealth of research, depth of analysis and provocative insight. Its distinctive feature, however, is the depth of emotion and existential passion that comes through on almost every page. One does not have to agree with every detail of his argument to be convinced of his essential thesis that ". . . lament and joy, faith and doubt, clarity and ambiguity, belong together in Christian living." *Sarah's Laughter* is intellectually convincing, spiritually nourishing, and of burning relevance to the times in which we live, and hence a must-read for every genuine person of faith!

Rev Ivan Satyavrata, PhD
Senior Pastor and Chairman,
The Assembly of God Church and Mission, Kolkata, India

To all his writings, Vinoth Ramachandra brings passion, theological acumen and constant sensitivity to life's realities. In this rich and sobering study, his experiences of bloody conflict and injustice in society and domestic politics, and of suffering and grief in personal life, are integrated into these qualities. The reader who is determined to learn rather than insist on agreeing with every jot and tittle will come away from this book informed, chastened and with a more realistic understanding of Christian faith which will strengthen Christian life and thought.

Stephen Williams, PhD
Honorary Professor of Theology,
Queen's University, Belfast, UK

Christians schooled in the kind of cozy discipleship where life with God is always bright and cheery need the prophetic realism that this book brings. It offers an eloquent dissection of human pain and suffering and invites us to acknowledge and embrace them in God's presence. The author laments the disappearance of lament in worship and argues for a theological appreciation of God as one who suffers for and with his people. The God presented in these pages is not a detached and impervious deity, but one who is actively responsive to human pain and suffering. Here is a call to faithful waiting for God's future salvation, the certain coming of which galvanizes us to action in the world to address the root causes of unjust suffering and needless death. Readers will surely come away stretched in their thinking, warmed in their hearts, and challenged in their commitment.

Mark L. Y. Chan, PhD
Earnest Lau Professor of Systematic Theology,
Trinity Theological College, Singapore

When my husband was murdered, I could not read but one of the books I was gifted. Nicholas Wolterstorff's *Lament for a Son* accompanied me by voicing my inarticulate grief. No doubt Ramachandra's *Sarah's Laughter* will serve equally as welcome company to all who yearn to retain faith while remaining honest to personal and societal pain. In evocatively true-to-life strokes and theological depth, Vinoth portrays the unvarnished complexities of human questioning and hope in the midst of human and creational loss and longing, lament and joy, light and darkness. This book accompanies us as we walk through pain, rather than skirting it, so that we may open up to God's restorative work.

Ruth Padilla DeBorst, PhD
Resonate Global Mission
International Fellowship of Mission as Transformation (INFEMIT)

Sarah's Laughter

Doubt, Tears, and Christian Hope

Vinoth Ramachandra

Published 2020 by Langham Global Library
An imprint of Langham Publishing
www.langhampublishing.org

Langham Publishing and its imprints are a ministry of Langham Partnership

Langham Partnership
PO Box 296, Carlisle, Cumbria, CA3 9WZ, UK
www.langham.org

ISBNs:
978-1-78368-857-9 Print
978-1-78368-858-6 ePub
978-1-78368-859-3 Mobi
978-1-78368-860-9 PDF

British Library Cataloguing-in-Publication Data
A catalogue record for this book is available from the British Library

ISBN: 978-1-78368-857-9

Cover & Book Design: projectluz.com

In loving memory of Karin,
whose courage and self-giving lifestyle
inspired many around the world.

Contents

1

Why, O Lord, Do You Hide Your Face?

Those who believe they believe in God, but without passion in their hearts, without anguish of mind, without uncertainty, without doubt, and even at times without despair, believe only in the idea of God, not in God Himself.[1]

Grief, Silence and Selective Amnesia

How long, LORD, must I call for help,
    but you do not listen?
Or cry to you, "Violence!"
    but you do not save?
Why do you make me look at injustice?
    Why do you tolerate wrongdoing?
Destruction and violence are before me;
    there is strife, and conflict abounds.
Therefore the law is paralysed,
    and justice never prevails.
The wicked hem in the righteous,
    so that justice is perverted . . .
    Why are you silent while the wicked
    swallow up those more righteous than themselves?
(Hab 1:2–4, 13)

1. Miguel de Unamuno (1864–1936), "The Tragic Sense of Life," in *Men and Nations*, trans. A. Kerrigan (London: Routledge and Kegan Paul, 1972), 211.

The words of Habakkuk were constantly on my lips during the bloody civil war in Sri Lanka that began in the early 1980s and came to a brutal end only in 2009. What had begun as a legitimate struggle for civil rights in the 1950s by the minority Tamil community in the north, and later developed into a violent demand for a separate Tamil state, quickly descended into a protracted "tit for tat" spiral of revenge. More than one hundred thousand people lost their lives and countless others lost their homes and fled the country as refugees.[2]

As is customary in such violent conflicts, appalling atrocities and massive human rights abuses were committed by both the Tamil separatist guerrillas and the armed forces. None of the grievances that led to the war have yet been addressed, nor have those who were responsible for war crimes and human rights abuses been brought to justice. Sri Lanka is only one among a number of countries – often rich in natural beauty and boasting a proud cultural and religious heritage – which have been ruined by venal and incompetent politicians and power-hungry religious nationalists. There are also a number of "forgotten wars" which, at any instant in time, are being waged around the world but rarely are reported in the global news channels, let alone on social media.

Conflict-prone states are often enormously rich in resources. This has led some development economists to speak of these countries as suffering from the "resource curse." The combination of weak governance and huge natural resources that offer the promise of speedy lucre to those who control their production and export is a major cause of violent conflicts. Diamonds in Angola and Sierra Leone, timber and diamonds in Liberia, gems in Afghanistan, and copper, gold, cobalt and timber in the Democratic Republic of the Congo have all been at the centre of civil conflict. The Grasberg mine in West Papua, the largest gold mine and second largest copper mine in the world, is owned by Freeport McMoran and Rio Tinto in one of the poorest regions of Indonesia which is now seeing the rise of a separatist guerrilla struggle. Angola boasts the second largest oil reserves in Africa and the fourth largest diamond reserves in the world. Its massive natural wealth was used to fuel a civil war that killed or maimed a million people between 1975 and 2002 and left another four million internally displaced. Three years after the end of the war, it ranked 160 out of

2. For more on the war in Sri Lanka, see my *Subverting Global Myths: Theology and the Public Issues Shaping Our World* (London: SPCK; Downers Grove, IL: IVP Academic, 2008), 69–72.

177 countries on the Human Development Index of the United Nations, with a life expectancy of forty years.[3]

The full cost of such conflicts cannot be captured by statistics alone (and, in any case, data are often least reliable in countries undergoing violent conflict). The immediate human costs, though enormous, represent a small fraction of the price countries pay for conflict. In protracted conflicts, whole generations of children and youth are brutalized by the effects of war. Families and communities pass on the trauma of rape, looting and violent deaths to posterity. Natural habitats are devastated, and food production and local markets are disrupted, leading to widespread malnutrition and undermining gains made in health and education.

Violent conflict gives rise to chain reactions that extend the suffering of ordinary people. Schoolteachers and medical personnel flee conflict areas, thereby worsening the conditions for those left behind. The latter have no option but to join rebel groups or volunteer for the army in the hope of scraping a meagre living. A slowing economy and an uncertain security environment represent powerful disincentives for investment, domestic and foreign, and a powerful incentive for capital flight on the part of local elites.

Women and children are especially vulnerable. Women suffer the brutality of rape and abuse, both during and after conflict. In recent years mass rape during war has been documented in Bosnia and Herzegovina, Cambodia, Liberia, Peru, Somalia and Uganda. Many of these women continue to suffer from serious long-term trauma which is compounded by ostracization at the hands of family and the wider community. It is now recognized that violence against women is an institutionalized strategy adopted by warring factions, including government forces, in many situations of conflict.

People in rich countries are directly linked to communities in poor countries where lives are being devastated by conflict. International drug trafficking and illicit arms transfers provide the financing and the weapons that fuel violent conflicts. The USA, the UK and some other Western European governments are the biggest arms traders in the world, often selling expensive military technology to countries that have a poor record of democracy and respect for human rights. The entry of refugees and asylum seekers on the doorstep of the rich fuels widespread racism and xenophobia in rich nations and leads to a breakdown in community relations. The illicit fortunes of those

---

3. *United Nations Human Development Report 2005* (New York: UNDP, 2005), 167. The HDI is a summary measure for assessing long-term progress in three basic dimensions of human development: a long and healthy life, access to knowledge and a decent standard of living.

who make massive profits from war and local conflicts are often stored in the international banking system owned and controlled by the rich nations of the world, or in tax havens which are protectorates of the USA and the UK.

Historical amnesia is what we are up against, wherever we happen to live, in our educational systems no less than in the mass media. Many American Christians are brought up on myths about the superiority of their political institutions and America's anti-imperial "essence." Hence the political naïveté that marks so much of American church life and seminary education. Many find it impossible to believe that they are ruled by an oligarchy, and so they have supported illegal aggression and sat idle while their constitutional safeguards against arbitrary executive power have been shredded. They cannot see connections between, say, the US involvement in the Middle East and the way that Texas and large parts of Mexico were annexed in the 1840s in order to wrest the monopoly of cotton – which was the nineteenth-century Industrial Revolution's equivalent of oil.

Histories, whether of nations or of organizations, are not only forgotten, they are sometimes officially erased. The only war crimes schoolchildren learn about are those of their defeated foes, not of the victors. The furore raised in China and Korea over the "whitewashing" in Japanese school textbooks of Japanese atrocities during the Second World War has been widely covered in the British and American media. But the latter have been largely silent over the massive scale of war crimes the British and American air forces committed against German and Japanese civilian populations in that same war. It is now becoming apparent that heavily populated cities were deliberately targeted by the Allies for "saturation bombing."

Robert McNamara's frank but belated revelations in the 2004 film documentary *The Fog of War* detail how he and other defence planners sought to maximize Japanese civilian casualties at minimal cost. Having little in the way of air defences, Japanese cities provided soft targets to US bombers. Four months before the atomic devastation of Hiroshima and Nagasaki in August 1945, most of Tokyo was razed to the ground in a hellish firestorm generated by sustained American bombing. More than one hundred thousand people lost their lives. Tokyo was selected as a target precisely because it was very densely populated and made mostly of wood.

McNamara quotes General Curtis LeMay, with whom he served during the firebombing of Japanese cities, as saying, "If we'd lost the war, we'd all have been prosecuted as war criminals." McNamara himself admitted: "I think he's right . . . But what makes it immoral if you lose and not immoral if you win?" The bombing of densely populated urban centres, even when there were no military targets, was removed from the category of war crimes at the Nuremberg and Tokyo trials, simply because the Allies did it much more than the Axis powers.[4] The same McNamara went on to be the Defence Secretary during the worst years of the Vietnam war, overseeing the destruction of large parts of that and neighbouring countries. His faithful service to the US military-corporate system was rewarded by his being appointed Director of the World Bank, his last major career move.

The term "fake news" has been in wide circulation since the rise of Donald Trump to the American presidency in 2016. However, misinformation and deliberate disinformation have long been practised by governments everywhere, not least by those which set themselves up as paragons of democracy. Winston Churchill was voted the "greatest Briton of the twentieth century" in a popular survey conducted at the beginning of the new millennium. Churchill was blatantly racist and imperialistic; and he observed in a private paper submitted to his cabinet colleagues in January 1914: "We are not a young people with *an innocent record and* a scanty inheritance. We have engrossed to ourselves . . . an *altogether disproportionate* share of the wealth and traffic of the world. We have got all we want in territory, and our claim to be left in the unmolested employment of vast and splendid possessions, *mainly acquired by violence, largely maintained by force*, often seems less reasonable to others than to us." However, when Churchill made this same paper public in the 1920s, in his book *The World Crisis*, he deliberately removed the italicized phrases which would have offended his reading public.[5]

The same selective amnesia attends media discussions about racism in Europe. To equate the racism of white supremacists today with Nazism, and to allude to the latter as if it were an aberration in European history, contrary to "European values," is to ignore the long history of Spanish and Portuguese conquistadors; nineteenth-century German xenophobia and their colonial atrocities in East and South-West Africa; the Belgian rape of the Congo; or the white supremacist assumptions of many Enlightenment thinkers and the French, Dutch and British colonial administrators from North Africa to the Pacific islands.

4. Noam Chomsky, *Imperial Ambitions: Conversations on the Post-9/11 World* (New York: Metropolitan Books, 2005), 65–68.

5. Clive Ponting, *Churchill* (London: Sinclair-Stevenson, 1994), 132.

The Questions of Grief

We are angered not only by horrendous acts of human cruelty and deceit, but also by the callous slaughter of animals and the destruction of habitats. Year upon year, thousands of fires rage in the Amazon rainforest, the "lung" of the planet and home to the richest source of biodiversity. The fires are started by ignorant peasant cultivators working for soya bean exporters, and multinational logging and mining conglomerates hand-in-glove with a far-right government. Climate change leaves a trail of devastation all over the world: from record high temperatures and intense storms in North America, Western Europe and Australia to severe, unseasonal flooding in India and South-East Asia. Not to mention disappearing forest cover, desertification and accelerating biodiversity loss everywhere from Brazil through sub-Saharan Africa to Indonesia. Even as our technological prowess increases at a staggering pace, we are becoming more aware of our fragility and vulnerability as a human species.

In October 2018, I visited an exhibition in London commemorating the centenary of the 1918–19 influenza pandemic that affected nearly a third of the world's population. The origins of the flu virus remain controversial, but an overcrowded military camp and hospital in France, which treated thousands of victims of chemical attacks and other casualties of the First World War, was a major site for its transmission. Massive movements of troops, many debilitated by combat and malnourishment and consequently more susceptible to infection, hastened the pandemic; and British and French troops returning to their colonial outposts around the world increased the spread and augmented mutations of the virus. It is estimated that anywhere between fifty million and one hundred million people all over the world died as a result of the pandemic, far outnumbering the combined deaths of both world wars and making it the greatest "medical holocaust" in human history. The deaths included eighteen million in India and four million in Africa. These were people who had nothing to do with the war.[6]

The statistics are mind-boggling. But the audio recordings of people expressing bewilderment and terror as they struggled to care for their sick family members were also heart-rending. This was before the discovery of vaccines, antiviral drugs and antibiotics; and people bathed patients in alcohol thinking this would eliminate the infection. The worst-affected individuals succumbed to a condition called cyanosis that saw their lips, cheeks and ears turn a purple-blue colour as their lungs filled with choking fluids. I found

6. See Centers for Disease Control and Prevention, "1918 Pandemic (H1N1 Virus)," https://www.cdc.gov/flu/pandemic-resources/1918-pandemic-h1n1.html.

myself struggling with the perennial question: Where was God in all this innocent suffering, apart from in the heroic actions of nurses and doctors who sacrificed themselves to save other lives? Also, why did the advent of vaccines and antibiotics appear so late in human history? What meaning do traditional Christian doctrines such as the "sovereignty of God" or "the providence of God" carry in situations such as these?

Even as I write, a novel coronavirus SARS-CoV-2 (resulting in an illness known as COVID-19) is spreading across the globe, with terrible long-term consequences. The elderly and those suffering from underlying health conditions are especially at risk. The hardest hit, from both the virus and the measures taken by governments to contain it, are the poor, vulnerable communities in every nation. Those who survive on daily wages will not receive economic bail-outs. For many poor countries a slowing of the economy spells the collapse of their already fragile health systems, resulting in more deaths, not only from Covid-19 but from hunger and other illnesses as well. The pandemic has exposed the exploited and unappreciated underclasses on whose labour the rest of us are dependent. It is tragically ironic that the very people whom affluent societies routinely ignore – migrant farm workers, those providing social care and cleaning services, hospital nurses and orderlies, supermarket attendants, etc. – are at the frontline of managing the pandemic; while the people whom the media obsess over – the celebrities, politicians, bankers, and CEOs – steal away on their private jets to their luxury villas where they can self-isolate.

Infectious disease specialists have been warning world governments for a long time about such impending crises, and the World Health Organization had encouraged countries to ensure that they met minimum standards for pandemic preparedness long before COVID-19. In 2018, it detected outbreaks of six of its eight "priority diseases" for the very first time. Instead of empowering the United Nations and the WHO, the rise of populist nationalism in recent decades has led to governments starving these institutions of the financial resources and authority they need to safeguard global public good. So, while pandemics are a result of our global interconnectedness, they are exacerbated by our lack of global cooperation.[7]

On a personal level, my wife Karin died six months before my visit to the 1918–19 influenza exhibition in London. In her last sermon in our church just before Christmas 2017, she framed her illness from cancer and impending

7. See, *The Conversation*, "The World before This Coronavirus and after Cannot Be the Same," https://theconversation.com/the-world-before-this-coronavirus-and-after-cannot-be-the-same-134905.

death within the story of Mary's Song (the Magnificat): the Saviour who will one day turn the world right-side up, but meanwhile we have to live with many unanswered questions. Mary embraced the social stigma of being an unmarried mother as well as the prospect of losing her son to an early death. Most of us ask, "Why me?" when affliction suddenly comes upon us; but, as Karin pointed out, we should be asking instead, "Why *not* me?" After all, we live in a messed-up world where men, women and children die every minute from accident, violence, illness, famine or natural disasters. Christ never promised us immunity from these. As Christians, we are part of a suffering humanity that still awaits redemption.

But the questions of grief can be tormenting, often even incapacitating. And grief arises not only with the loss of a loved one to death, but with the loss of health, employment and reputation; with infertility and disability; and, furthermore, with the painful realization that injustice and wickedness often go unchecked. In the Second Epistle of Peter, we read of Lot, the nephew of Abraham, living in the ancient cities of Sodom and Gomorrah, being "distressed by the depraved conduct of the lawless (for that righteous man, living among them day after day, was tormented in his righteous soul by the lawless deeds he saw and heard)" (2 Pet 2:7–8).

There is a long, rich and oft-ignored tradition of lament that runs through the Bible. It begins with the startling words in the early chapters of Genesis attributed to God himself: "The LORD saw how great the wickedness of the human race had become on the earth, and that every inclination of the thoughts of the human heart was only evil all the time. The LORD regretted that he had made human beings on the earth, and his heart was deeply troubled" (Gen 6:5–6). It culminates in the cry of the martyrs around the throne of God in the vision of John the Seer: "How long, Sovereign Lord, holy and true, until you judge the inhabitants of the earth and avenge our blood?" (Rev 6:10).

The two questions that are uppermost in the lament tradition are "Why, Lord?" and "How long, O Lord?" But the question "Why?" is not a call for a theoretical explanation of suffering and evil. It is an expression of existential anguish over the silence and inaction of God in the face of threat, disaster or unmitigated suffering. It is really the question, "Why, Lord, are you hidden, indifferent or absent?" The sting in innocent suffering for the believer is not the pain itself nor the injustice of it, but the sense of God-forsakenness. This is what is unendurable. Trust in God has been weakened. Is God's power limited to acts of vindication in the past or can he still be trusted to make a difference in the world today?

More than a third of the Psalms, which was the hymnbook of ancient Israel and the early church, are categorized as psalms of lament. They express confusion, distress, pain, indignation, fear, outrage and protest, as a result of either individual suffering or collective humiliation and oppression. Whereas for the prophets, human sin is the root cause of lament, frequently in the Psalms there is no reliable connection between suffering and sin. Typical is Psalm 44:20–26:

> If we had forgotten the name of our God
> or spread out our hands to a foreign god,
> would not God have discovered it,
> since he knows the secrets of the heart?
> Yet for your sake we face death all day long;
> we are considered as sheep to be slaughtered.
> Awake, Lord! Why do you sleep?
> Rouse yourself! Do not reject us for ever.
> Why do you hide your face
> and forget our misery and oppression?
> We are brought down to the dust;
> our bodies cling to the ground.
> Rise up and help us;
> rescue us because of your unfailing love.

Or consider the socio-political criticism of Psalm 10:1–4, 12:

> Why, LORD, do you stand far off?
> Why do you hide yourself in times of trouble?
> In his arrogance the wicked man hunts down the weak,
> who are caught in the schemes he devises.
> He boasts about the cravings of his heart;
> he blesses the greedy and reviles the LORD.
> In his pride the wicked man does not seek him;
> in all his thoughts there is no room for God . . .
> Arise, LORD! Lift up your hand, O God.
> Do not forget the helpless.

And the cry of personal affliction in Psalm 88, perhaps the bleakest of all the psalms:

> Is your love declared in the grave,
> your faithfulness in Destruction?

Are your wonders known in the place of darkness,
    or your righteous deeds in the land of oblivion?
But I cry to you for help, LORD;
    in the morning my prayer comes before you.
Why, LORD, do you reject me
    and hide your face from me?
From my youth I have suffered and been close to death;
    I have borne your terrors and am in despair.
Your wrath has swept over me;
    your terrors have destroyed me.
All day long they surround me like a flood;
    they have completely engulfed me.
You have taken from me friend and neighbour –
    darkness is my closest companion.
(vv. 11–18)

Lament is the verbalizing of raw pain, the bringing to speech of suffering. It is not unbelief, but honest and faithful speech that keeps the conversation with God going when the psalmist and his community experience not the promised land of peace and blessing but the wasteland of meaninglessness and oppression. "It is the bitter complaint of one who despairs, who has no one else to whom he can turn. He clings to God against God . . . Doubt about God, even the kind of despair that can no longer understand God, receives in the lament a language that binds it to God, even as it accuses him."[8]

Walter Brueggemann writes about these psalms:

> The use of these "psalms of darkness" may be judged by the world to be acts of *unfaith and failure*, but for the trusting community, their use is *an act of bold faith*, albeit a transformed faith. It is an act of bold faith on the one hand, because it insists that the world must be experienced as it really is and not in some pretended way. On the other hand, it is bold because it insists that all such experiences of disorder are a proper subject for discourse with God.[9]

That is why no questions are "off-limits," no speech addressed to God deemed too "uncivil" or "impolite" for prayer. The psalmist believes in a God who is big enough to handle his doubts, protests and even his rage.

---

8. Claus Westermann, "The Role of the Lament in the Theology of the Old Testament," *Interpretation* 28 (Jan. 1974): 34.

9. Walter Brueggemann, *The Message of the Psalms* (Minneapolis, MN: Augsburg Press, 1984), 52.

Thus, as another Old Testament scholar, Scott Ellington, also observes, lament presupposes a relationship of trust and intimacy. "When the biblical writers lament, they do so from within the context of a foundational relationship that binds together the individual with members of the community of faith and that community with their God."[10] It is precisely because the one who laments believes in a God who has bound himself in covenantal love to his people, and is indeed good, just and compassionate, that the injustice and terror he or she experiences and the accompanying silence of God occasion such bewilderment and heartfelt anguish. For those who do not believe in such a God, expressions of impotent rage at the fact of innocent suffering are a mere howling in the wind, an outpouring of venom into an impersonal, uncaring void.

And yet it is curious how so many professedly atheist writers do, in fact, experience and express such outrage in the face of injustice. John Fowles, the existentialist novelist, wrote after the death of his wife Elizabeth: "As an atheist, it made me very angry with someone – He, She, or It – who doesn't exist."[11] The self-confessed irony here lies in the fact that the rage against death and the yearning for ultimate meaningfulness to our life stories are fundamentally religious impulses. If men and women believed themselves to be mere flotsam in an accidental universe, or that God was neither good, loving, nor powerful, there would, presumably, be no moral and spiritual torment to undergo. Their suffering would simply be a brute fact of the world, nothing more. But so-called secular men and women continue to experience not only bewilderment but also a sense of moral outrage in the face of innocent suffering. It seems their outrage arises precisely because they believe, at levels deeper than conscious thought, that their universe *is* fundamentally ordered, meaningful and good. The silence of God is hardest to bear for those who believe in a living God who relates personally to the human creation, and is not an amoral, inscrutable process.

The telling of Israel's story of redemption formed the interpretative framework within which the people of Israel understood themselves and their world. It was their foundational narrative. They retold that story in the context of lament to remind God of his covenant promises. They are the grounds of their appeal to God to intervene. Thus, the opening cry of abandonment in Psalm 22, found on the lips of Jesus himself as he hung on the cross, "My God, my God, why have you forsaken me? Why are you so far from saving me, so far from my cries of anguish?" is followed by the memory of past divine acts:

10. Scott A. Ellington, *Risking Truth: Reshaping the World through Prayers of Lament* (Eugene, OR: Pickwick, 2008), 7.

11. Quoted in his obituary, *Guardian Weekly*, 18–24 November 2005.

In you our ancestors put their trust;
    they trusted and you delivered them.
To you they cried out and were saved;
    in you they trusted and were not put to shame.
(Ps 22:4–5)

Many of these lament psalms, including the one above, are punctuated by outbreaks of praise and thanksgiving, the psalmist assuring himself and the community to which he belongs of God's goodness and faithfulness (22:23–28; see too 10:16–17). This seeming contradiction has led some commentators to suppose that these are later interpolations by editors troubled by the unanswered cry of despair, or that these psalms are a patchwork of fragments assembled without any sense of coherence. But all who have experienced bereavement know that such emotional fluctuations are part and parcel of the grief process. Mood swings are the roller coaster on which many of us ride. Moreover, the language of lament enables the one who grieves to articulate the contradictions of experience. The God who is absent is, at the same time, the only God who can save.

The psalms of lament, when appropriated today in our individual and collective prayers, allow us to be honest; and honesty is the most basic aspect of prayer. But they also effect a transformation in us. Esther de Waal puts it this way:

> As we pray or sing, or shout them, the psalms use the strong language which does not try to pretend that we are nice. So we can groan, complain bitterly, tell God how unfair his actions are, indulge in bitter grief and reveal all our mental hurts and despair. All the sadnesses that wash over us, and all the feelings of anger and resentment, all those violent feelings, and not least when they become ugly and bitter, are here expressed without any apology or pretence. Even the saying of these hateful things out loud is a way of acknowledging them, and of turning them over to God. If we know that we are being listened to by this God then we are at least standing in a place where God's healing can also begin.[12]

But for this transformation to begin, it is important that one not only give voice to one's suffering but that one owns it, makes it part of one's narrative identity. Nicholas Wolterstorff writes:

12. Esther de Waal, *Lost in Wonder: Rediscovering the Spiritual Art of Attentiveness* (Toronto: Novalis, 2003), 110.

> If someone asks, "Tell me who you are," one says, maybe not immediately but eventually, "I am someone who went through a painful divorce," "I am someone who suffered the loss of a child," "I am someone who was fired after twenty years of faithful work." To disown one's suffering is to try to delete it from one's narrative or prevent it from ever becoming a part – to try to forget it, put it behind one, get on with things. Lament, in requiring that one voice one's suffering, requires that one not only name it but own it.[13]

Wolterstorff, who is one of the leading Christian philosophical theologians of our time, lost his own son in a mountaineering accident and wrote a moving reflection on his grief, entitled *Lament for a Son*. His honesty shines forth on every page, such as in the following confession of his inability to make sense of his loss:

> I have no explanation. I can do nothing else than endure in the face of this deepest and most painful of mysteries. I believe in God the Father Almighty, the maker of heaven and earth, and the resurrection of Jesus Christ. I also believe that my son's life was cut short in its prime. I cannot fit these pieces together. I am at a loss. I have read the theodicies produced to justify the ways of God to man. I find them unconvincing. To the most agonized question I have ever asked I do not know the answer. I do not know why God would watch him fall. I do not know why God would watch me wounded. I cannot even guess . . . I am not angry but baffled and hurt. My wound is an unanswered question. The wounds of all humanity are an unanswered question.[14]

The Kenyan theologian Jesse Mugambi laments the state of his continent, asking the searching question, "How can we explain the apparent contradiction, that contemporary Africa continues to be, perhaps the most religious continent in the world, and yet its peoples remain the most abused of all in history? How could it be that peoples who continue to call on God most reverently are the ones whom God seems to neglect most vehemently? Could it be that irreligion is the key to success, and that religion is the key to backwardness?"[15]

---

13. Nicholas Wolterstorff, "If God Is Good and Sovereign, Why Lament?," in Nicholas Wolterstorff, *Hearing the Call: Liturgy, Justice, Church and World*, ed. Mark R. Gornik and Gregory Thompson (Grand Rapids, MI: Eerdmans, 2011), 81.

14. Nicholas Wolterstorff, *Lament for a Son* (Grand Rapids, MI: Eerdmans, 1987), 67–68.

15. Jesse Mugambi, *From Liberation to Reconstruction: African Christian Theology after the Cold War* (Nairobi: East African Educational Publishers, 1995), 33.

In similar vein, Archbishop Desmond Tutu, writing in the era of apartheid in South Africa, raises the stark, oft-neglected issue of the church's complicity in political crimes. "The perplexity we have to deal with is this: why does suffering single out black people so conspicuously, suffering not at the hands of pagans and other believers, but at the hands of fellow Christians who claim allegiance to the same Lord and Master?"[16]

Contemporary Lament

Music, art and poetry have been impacted over time by the tradition of biblical lament. Those inspired by Western classical music can point to the works of Johann Sebastian Bach, especially his *St Matthew's Passion*. The late symphonies and string quartets of the twentieth-century Russian composer Dmitri Shostakovich, who struggled to make any sense of life in the horrific decades of Stalinist terror, have been a source of great comfort to those experiencing the disorientation of personal grief.[17] And, of course, one can never forget the spirituals of African American slaves on the cotton plantations of the American South, the progenitor of jazz.[18]

The psalms of lament have inspired several modern Christian poets to articulate their own anguish in contemporary psalms. The following are some examples. The first is from the Nicaraguan Catholic priest and poet Ernesto Cardenal:

> My God, my God, oh why hast thou forsaken me?
> I am but the travesty of a man
> despised of the people
> laughed into scorn in every daily paper.
> Their armoured cars encompass me,
> their machine-gunners have set their sights on me,

---

16. Desmond Tutu, *The Voice of One Crying in the Wilderness* (London, 1982), 35; quoted in John Parratt, *Reinventing Christianity: African Theology Today* (Grand Rapids, MI: Eerdmans; Trenton, NJ: Africa World Press, 1995), 155.

17. Personal communication with David Smith, as well as the closing paragraphs of his *Stumbling towards Zion* (Carlisle: Langham Global Library, 2019). Smith comments that, although not a Christian, Shostakovich was deeply influenced by the biblical Psalms as well as by Jewish folk songs. His Seventh Symphony (the "Leningrad") was composed and first performed in Leningrad during the terrible siege by the German army in the depths of a bone-chilling Russian winter. Shostakovich's Eighth Symphony, a threnody for the victims of the Second World War, is a cathartic experience even for those who have never experienced war.

18. Nancy Lee has collected several laments from diverse cultures and religions in Nancy C. Lee, *Lyrics of Lament: From Tragedy to Transformation* (Minneapolis, MN: Fortress, 2010). I confine myself here to laments inspired directly by biblical texts.

Barbed wire besets me round.
From morning until evening
I must answer to my name;
They have tattooed me with a number.
They have photographed me
hedged about with an electric fence.
My bones may all be told on an X-ray screen.
They have taken my identity away from me.
They have led me naked to the gas-chamber;
and they have parted my garments among them –
yea even down to my shoes.
I call out for morphia but no one hears;
I call out in the strait-jacket,
Call out all night long in lunatic asylums –
in the ward for terminal cases,
in the isolation wing,
in the home for the aged.
Drenched in sweat, I suffer
in the psychiatric clinic, stifle
In the oxygen tent, and weep
In the police station,
in the prison yard,
in the torture chamber,
in the orphanage;
I am contaminated by radioactivity
and all men shun me lest it might smite them.[19]

The American poet Ann Weems wrote a book of fifty personal psalms following the death of her son in an act of violence. Here are excerpts from two of them:

I don't know where to look for you, O God!
I've called and I've called.
I've looked and I've looked.
I go back to my room
And sit in the dark
Waiting for you.
Could you give me a sign

---

19. Ernesto Cardenal, *Marilyn Monroe and Other Poems*, trans. Robert Pring-Mill (London: Search Press, 1975), 79–80.

That you've heard?
Could you numb my emotions
So I wouldn't hurt so much?[20]

How long will you watch, O God,
as your people live huddled in death?
The whole world
is distressed in tears,
and I have joined
the procession of the bereaved
who walk daily in the dark place.
We drown in the sea.
We bleed on the battlefield.
We lie stricken on sickbeds.
We are judged in the courtrooms.
We are victims of crime.
We are homeless and hungry.
Is this not enough? . . .

We watch our loved ones endure pain.
We are falsely accused.
We encounter prejudice and hate.
We are humiliated and abused.
We contend with unbearable stress and anxiety.
We weep by the grave . . .

Look upon us
and let your heart be moved
to break the bonds of the bereaved.
In this hope is our joy.
In that day we will run
to join the procession of life
and we will sing hymns of praise
Forever and ever
and ever
and ever![21]

20. Ann Weems, *Psalms of Lament* (Louisville, KY: Westminster John Knox Press, 1995), 43. Used with permission.

21. Weems, *Psalms of Lament*, 65–67. Used with permission.

Finally, from the killing fields of Jaffna, northern Sri Lanka, written by an Anglican clergyman, Fr. Selvan, during the height of the war and based on Revelation 6:10:

How long will we wait – O Sovereign Lord,
How long will we wait?
How long will we wait for those who killed
and destroyed us to repent?
How long will we wait?

We lived by farming – helped
Many poor to live.
Why did the missiles detonate? – Why did they
Finish us off? – How long . . .

We lived by fishing – provided
Many with their food.
We were arrested – we did
Perish to the ground – How long . . .

We were teaching – became the
Instruments of learning
Got struck by the land mines – became
Corpses in an instant – How long . . . [22]

About a quarter of the biblical psalms of lament are collective in form (written in the first-person plural); but even the "I" of the individual laments serves a representative function, modelling for the community how to express grief and resolve doubt. We do not know the original music to which the communal psalms were sung, but the fact that they were written to be sung is instructive. Music is evocative as well as expressive, connecting deeply with our emotions. It enables the honest articulation of sorrow as well as helps towards the awakening of hope. There is ample testimony from cultures all over the world that music can minister to people who experience dementia or bereavement in ways in which words often fail. Lamenting together also binds people to each other, as does collective singing in general (it is not accidental that all protest marches against injustice and oppression involve the singing of songs). It is what the greatest hymns of the church do, inspiring communal faith and courage.

22. With kind permission of the author. The rhythms have been lost in translation from the Tamil.

Jeremy Begbie, a musician and professor of theology, elaborates on this:

> This is why people who grieve often do not want cheerful music, nor something that just plays the chaos of their grief back to them, and not even something that simply concentrates their grief (important as this is). Instead they want something that can both connect with their grief and help them find new forms of grief, perhaps forms that help set their sorrow in a larger, more hopeful emotional context. Is this not just what the best funeral music should be doing?[23]

The Ugandan theologian Emmanuel Katongole has collected a number of poetic and musical laments from parts of Africa where human suffering has been immense. In the book *Born from Lament* he shows that the verbalizing of pain by men and women has political agency in that it leads to a rebirth of hope and the will to resist:

> Lament is agency. The ground on which the faith activists stand is a ground of immense pain and suffering, a reality that has been captured through a number of poems, songs, and other cultural expressions from Congo and northern Uganda. These activists are caught up within this vortex of suffering. Their agency is in the first place a cry of lament . . . far from passively acquiescing to suffering, lament is an active engagement with the world of suffering. Far from distracting us from practical engagement, the practice of lament deepens and intensifies engagement with the world of suffering. Lament invites us into deeper political engagement, while at the same time reframing and reconstituting the very nature and meaning of politics.[24]

After the civil war in Sri Lanka ended traumatically with the defeat of the Tamil separatist guerrillas in the north, the government proclaimed it a victory in the "global fight against terror" and claimed that Sri Lanka was the first nation ever to "defeat terrorism."[25] The same political rhetoric, along with

23. Jeremy Begbie, *Resounding Truth: Christian Wisdom in the World of Music* (London: SPCK, 2007), 302.

24. Emmanuel Katongole, *Born from Lament: The Theology and Politics of Hope in Africa* (Grand Rapids, MI: Eerdmans, 2017), 261.

25. Of course, the Tamil Tigers used "terror" against their own people as well as the army and the majority population (suicide bombings, use of helpless civilians as shields, torture and assassination of dissident Tamils). But the armed forces also employed means that count as "terror": indiscriminate aerial bombardment and shelling of villages, extra-judicial killings, etc.

the self-description "war hero," was used to control the judiciary and the mass media, stifling all political dissent. At national Independence Day celebrations on 4 February every year, we were treated to long military parades and the same triumphalist propaganda. The factors that led to the war were ignored, and another opportunity for ethnic reconciliation squandered. In early 2013, I proposed to the Anglican synod that we mark that year's Independence Day celebration not with the traditional service of prayer for the nation, but with a "service of lament" over the political despotism and also over all who had perished in the war, whether they be soldiers, Tamil "terrorists," or civilians on all sides. Much to my surprise, the proposal was accepted unanimously. So a service of lament was held in the cathedral in Colombo as a counter to the patriotic fervour at the same time as the military parades. Many from other churches, as well as some Buddhist monks and other non-Christians disillusioned with the regime, joined us. The president of the country was incensed and issued threats which the bishops ignored. Less than two years later, the president was removed from power in an utterly unexpected and violence-free election.

Lamentless Churches

The Western church has used the Psalter as its hymnbook from earliest times. Augustine, Luther and Calvin wrote extensive commentaries on the Psalms, including the lament psalms. Augustine's largest single work was his *Enarrationes in Psalmos*, a collection of sermons on the Psalms, and in it he urged Christian congregations to use the psalmists' laments as their own words: "If the psalm prays, you pray; if it groans, you groan."[26] Luther's *Penitential Psalms* (1517) was his first original, published work; and the first book published in the American colonies was the *Bay Psalm Book* in 1640. The German pastor and martyr Dietrich Bonhoeffer cherished the Psalms as his principal form of prayer, both in solitude and in community. In a letter to his parents from his prison cell, he wrote: "I read the psalms every day, as I have done for years; I know them and love them more than any other book."[27]

26. Augustine, *Enarrationes in Psalmos* 30.2.3, cited in Rachel Ciano, "Lament Psalms in the Church," in *Finding Lost Words: The Church's Right to Lament*, ed. G. Geoffrey Harper and Kit Barker (Eugene, OR: Wipf & Stock, 2017), 11. Amongst possible reasons for the loss of lament in Western church worship since the eighteenth century, Ciano proposes the decline of belief in divine sovereignty, scientific explanations of suffering, and cultural stereotypes of "manliness."

27. Dietrich Bonhoeffer, *Letters and Papers from Prison*, Eng. trans. (London: SCM, 1953), letter of 15 May 1943, 18.

The virtual disappearance of lament from the pulpit, prayers and liturgies of churches in Asian churches that slavishly imitate the worship styles of affluent Western churches is a matter of grave concern, not least because it encourages dishonesty in our relationships with God and one another. Telling mothers who have lost their children not to grieve because "God is in control" or that "God is teaching them through suffering" is not only pastorally damaging but theologically shallow. Not only do we live in societies that are torn apart by ethnic and religious rivalries, and experience severe climatic events, growing economic disparities and corrupt politics, but we have many in our congregations who are crushed by these social realities as well as by domestic abuse, have nagging doubts about the trustworthiness of God's promises in Scripture or the relevance of the gospel for the cultural worlds they inhabit, and who struggle with unanswered prayer and the silence of God in the face of their deepest traumas. Such folk have no vocabulary with which to articulate their pain, because the biblical tradition of lament has been ignored in their churches. As the Singaporean pastor-theologian Gordon Wong has observed, "Our churches emphasise prayer and praise to God. But we almost always think that the only prayers acceptable to God are words of praise and thanksgiving."[28] It is not surprising, then, that many sensitive and thoughtful young people choose to "drop out" of church as their honest doubts and struggles are not being addressed.

Nancy Lee tells a story of a young Christian man traumatized by war that is all too common, wherever we may happen to live:

> In 1996, I was living in Croatia and traveling throughout much of Bosnia on a Fulbright fellowship during the year just after the wars ended. People were struggling with the traumas of the devastation of war. I commonly encountered examples of extraordinary faith and courage in the face of unspeakable hardship and horrors. A young man, who was a music minister at a Protestant church, confided to me one day that, at the time of the military draft, he had served in the army to defend his country during the war. His experience of the violence was devastating, and he was very troubled. The problem of war veterans falling into alcoholism due to their unprocessed trauma and grief was common. In that traditional eastern European culture, therapy was still seen as

28. Gordon Wong, *God, Why?: Habakkuk's Struggle with Faith in a World out of Control* (Singapore: Armour, 2007), 7.

> something taboo. The young man thought he might turn to the church and his pastor as a place where, through his music ministry, or song at least, he might find some solace for his own healing and also find a way to help others. When he suggested some sorrowful songs to the pastor, he was quickly dismissed and told that the church must emphasize positive music and the praise of God. At this rebuke, the young man fell into an unresolved despair laid on top of his inner, unprocessed trauma, and he painfully realized that his church's music was largely irrelevant for helping others who were as psychologically wounded as he was.[29]

To those who refuse to face the suffering of those amongst whom they live, or feel shame at their own vulnerabilities, the cries of lament seem so "unspiritual," embarrassing and even loathsome. And churches which suppress the biblical lament tradition in their preaching and liturgies are churches which are very much part of the status quo, having invested massively in the preservation of exploitative and oppressive social relations.

This tragic neglect of lament in our preaching and worship is more than a matter of ignorance; it is a lack of faith in the God of Scripture. A child who knows it is unconditionally loved by its parents enjoys the freedom to speak openly with them, expressing disappointment and anger as well as gratitude and love. We have noted that Old Testament Israel believed that the God of all creation had initiated a covenant with them, a covenant akin to a marriage relationship, and it was precisely this belief that allowed the prophets and hymn-writers of Israel to bring all their corporate and individual experiences of life into that relationship. Nothing was excluded. If, in times of pain and turmoil, we too know ourselves to be unconditionally loved by God, then we are free to question, challenge and even vent our anger at God. It is the security of love that engenders and emboldens lament.

The Australian pastor Malcolm Gill gives this advice to his fellow pastors: "To have a lament psalm read in church, even without comment, provides voice to those silently sinking under the weight of grief. To collectively recite a prayer of sorrow encourages the downcast that they are not the only ones bearing the burden of grief. Though quite rare, a musical lament via a traditional hymn or contemporary song can also verbalize the depths of pain when normal words can't be found."[30]

---

29. Lee, *Lyrics of Lament*, 14.

30. Malcolm J. Gill, "Praying Lament," in Harper and Barker, *Finding Lost Words*, 232–233.

Finally, for evangelical church leaders tempted by the lure of an entertainment culture, or simply afraid of the risks of exposure to the deep pain of the world, I commend the admonishment of Pope Francis in his encyclical *Evangelii Gaudium* ("The Joy of the Gospel"):

> I prefer a Church which is bruised, hurting and dirty because it has been out on the streets, rather than a Church which is unhealthy from being confined and from clinging to its own security . . . If something should rightly disturb and trouble our consciences, it is the fact that so many of our brothers and sisters are living without the strength, light and consolation born of friendship with Jesus Christ, without a community of faith to support them, without meaning and a goal in life. More than by fear of going astray, my hope is that we will be moved by the fear of remaining shut up within structures which give us a false sense of security, within rules which make us harsh judges, within habits which make us feel safe, while at our door people are starving and Jesus does not tire of saying to us: "Give them something to eat" (Mark 6:37).[31]

31. Pope Francis, *Evangelii Gaudium* (London: Catholic Truth Society, 2013), 29–30.

2

Job and the Messiness of Theology

> Talk to me about the truth of religion and I'll listen gladly. Talk to me about the duty of religion and I'll listen submissively. But don't come talking to me about the consolations of religion or I shall suspect that you don't understand.[1]

In his autobiographical reflections, the Jewish polymath George Steiner turns to the theme with which we began this book. He reminds us of the horrors that have been characteristic of every historical epoch. Judicial torture and the enslavement of the conquered, and the brutalization suffered by children and women in the hovels of urban slums or land owned by exploiting masters, have been perennial. "Recurrently, millions have subsisted on the constant edge of hunger, in habitations unfit even for animals, in illiteracy and a more or less conscious acceptance of disease, infant mortality, humiliation and early death . . . Killing-fields have followed on killing-fields. No period can boast of any novel or crowning inhumanity." In the twentieth century, he recalls that "Stalinism consigned its millions (seven, ten, fifteen?) to living burial in the mines of Kolyma, to planned starvation, to slow death by freezing and forced labour. It is said that the despot, during the blood-carnival of the great purges, signed up to 2,000 death-warrants *per diem*, sentences which meant the annihilation of whole families, the confinement of young children in state orphanages, the eradication of ethnic cultures."[2]

1. C. S. Lewis, *A Grief Observed* (London: Faber & Faber, 1961), 23.

2. George Steiner, *Errata: An Examined Life* (London: Weidenfeld & Nicolson, 1997), 103–106. For arguments for and against the view that the twentieth century was the most barbaric in history, see 103–109.

In the previous chapter, we saw that there is a world of difference between complaining *about* God and complaining *to* God. What is characteristic of biblical lament is that, unlike grumbling or harbouring silent resentment at God, it directly addresses God in prayer, however anguished, angry and despairing that prayer may be. This is because it is founded on the belief that God *does* care about his world, and that he *does* respond to the desperate prayers of his people. If Yahweh were a capricious deity, like the gods of the ancient Mediterranean world or the Indian subcontinent, lament would be a meaningless activity.

The practice of such lament arises whenever belief and experience collide. It holds together expectation and uncertainty, trust and questioning, belief in God's presence and the experience of his absence. The cry to Jesus of the father of the demon-possessed boy in Mark 9:24 ("I do believe; help me overcome my unbelief!") is in continuity with this tradition. The truth-claims of personal experience probe and sharpen our beliefs about God and the relationship we have with him; while our beliefs also shape our experiences, help interpret them and refuse to let them dictate to us. Scott Ellington puts this succinctly: "Faith is found neither in the repudiation of experience nor in the relinquishing of belief, but in addressing both truths in a creative tension before God. Thus, the prayer of lament is an act of faith. To lament is to risk the move towards newness, a move that is certain to reshape both our beliefs about God and our most formative experiences of him."[3]

The creative tension that Ellington mentions runs through the Old Testament book of Job. The latter is a theological drama, and like all great dramatic fiction enlarges our imagination by dismantling our conventional expectations and assumptions. The truths that it conveys are not black-and-white, well-defined propositions that can be summed up in coherent doctrinal statements and neat theological systems. God is Mystery, and his relationship to us and to his world is ultimately beyond our conceptual grasp. We can speak truthfully about him, in so far as he has revealed himself, but even in his self-revelation God remains hidden, beyond our comprehension.

The backdrop to the book of Job is a religious worldview familiar to those of us who inhabit Buddhist, Hindu or Muslim cultures. We reap what we sow; evil deeds bring forth their own negative, harmful consequences in the lives of the evildoer; the righteous are protected by God from suffering. In other words, bad things happen to bad people, good things to good people. This is also the

3. Scott A. Ellington, *Risking Truth: Reshaping the World through Prayers of Lament* (Eugene, OR: Pickwick, 2008), 15.

default theological position of many in our churches, as well as of otherwise sophisticated atheists when commenting on religious belief.

Stylistically, the book of Job comprises a prose frame (chapters 1–2; 42:7–17) enveloping a poetic core (chapters 3–42:6). The shocking dissonance between the frame and the core lies not in the styles but in their respective theologies. The opening narrative raises many puzzling questions. The reader is taken behind the curtain and told that Job's imminent afflictions are not the consequence of personal sin. They are the work of a *satan* (adversary), himself a servant of God, who is goaded by God and in turn manipulates God into a wager that results in the death of several innocent men, women and children. Having served his purpose in setting the stage, this *satan* makes no further appearance in the drama. What kind of God is this who sacrifices innocent lives for the sake of a wager with an underling?

The contrast between prose frame and poetic core has led many biblical scholars to surmise that the former represents an older tradition that has been adapted by the narrator to provide a counterpoint to the main arguments of the book. Job is presented as a patient saint in the introductory narrative, meekly submitting in the face of horrific tragedy with the words that are so typical of orthodox piety: "Naked I came from my mother's womb, and naked I shall depart. The LORD gave and the LORD has taken away; may the name of the LORD be praised" (Job 1:21). However, as Claus Westermann observes, the lament tradition which holds together contrasts encountered in personal experience offers a better way of understanding these tensions in the text. The messiness of the book of Job reflects the messiness of real life.

There are also passages of humble, serene trust (16:19–21; 19:25–27) woven into the main body of the work where Job refuses to conform his sufferings to any pious theological construct. "This is the solution to the two faces of Job. The pious, humble man, submissive to God's will, and the desperate man who resists God – these are one and the same person, in touch with both possibilities."[4] David Penchansky argues that it is *integrity*, not piety, that is central to the meaning of the book. "In the frame Job is on trial, and to maintain his integrity he must not curse God. In the centre God is on trial, and for Job to maintain his integrity, he must continue to assert his innocence, and God's guilt."[5]

---

4. Claus Westermann, "The Two Faces of Job," in *Job and the Silence of God*, ed. Christian Duquoc and Casiano Floristan, Concilium 169 (New York: Seabury, 1983), 15–22 (21–22).

5. David Penchansky, *The Betrayal of God: Ideological Conflict in Job* (Louisville, KY: Westminster John Knox Press, 1990), 47.

In a profound meditation on the difficult doctrine of divine providence, the Scottish theologian David Fergusson calls for a nuanced, indeed "polyphonic" approach to the subject. Providence denotes all the divine actions that are directed towards the good of God's creatures. These include creating, endowing, blessing, guiding, ruling, forgiving, reconciling, inspiring, prompting, healing, sanctifying and promising. "God's agency may be viewed as pluriform and differentiated, so that no one form of engagement with creation is privileged to the detriment of others." Different theological models are needed, each representing some particular aspect of scriptural teaching. Such a plurality of models "may lose some systematic coherence. But it may be better positioned to accommodate the diversity of scriptural materials that are reflected in the liturgical life of the church." Moreover, Fergusson suggests, "We might say that providence is a theological term that needs to be *narrated* through a series of descriptions of how God relates to creatures, rather than *defined* in any essentialist manner."[6]

Job's Anguish[7]

Job, then, is an upright and God-fearing man, living a respected, happy and prosperous life, who is suddenly plunged into sickness, deprivation and utter wretchedness. His friends find him seated on the garbage heap outside the city. He has been reduced, like so many in our modern world, to the status of a nonperson in the eyes of his wife, his friends and his former associates. His wife urges him to "Curse God and die!" (2:9). Will Job reject God? Was his faith and uprightness dependent on his material prosperity? If not, how will he now speak of God from the perspective of the garbage heap? These are the profound issues that the book unfolds. It raises the question whether there can be anything such as a disinterested faith, a faith "for nothing"; or whether all religious behaviour is finally motivated by selfish concerns.

In contrast to what the apostle James writes (Jas 5:11), the Job we meet beyond the second chapter of the book is not a patient man. And the book is not a call to patient endurance. Job is a rebellious believer. He protests his integrity and innocence to heaven. His righteous indignation is directed

6. David Fergusson, *The Providence of God: A Polyphonic Approach* (Cambridge: Cambridge University Press, 2018), 11, 298.

7. Much of the material that follows has been adapted and slightly expanded from the chapter "Job and the Silence of God," in my *Gods That Fail: Modern Idolatry and Christian Mission*, 2nd ed. (Eugene, OR: Wipf & Stock, 2016). Used by permission of Wipf & Stock Publishers. www.wipfandstock.com.

against a God who seems indifferent not only to his plight but also to the suffering of all innocent victims. He accuses God of arbitrariness in his dealings with humanity:

> If I say, "I will forget my complaint,
> I will change my expression and smile,"
> I still dread all my sufferings,
> for I know you will not hold me innocent.
> Since I am already found guilty,
> why should I struggle in vain?
> Even if I washed myself with soap
> and my hands with cleansing powder,
> you would plunge me into a slime pit
> so that even my clothes would detest me.
> (9:27–31)

So he longs for a mediator who will take up his cause and bring God to account:

> He is not a mere mortal like me that I might answer him,
> that we might confront each other in court.
> If only there were someone to mediate between us,
> someone to bring us together,
> someone to remove God's rod from me,
> so that his terror would frighten me no more.
> Then I would speak up without fear of him,
> but as it now stands with me, I cannot.
> (9:32–35)

Such language shocks his friends who represent the conventional wisdom of the day. Theirs is a neat theological scheme which makes perfect sense of Job's miserable situation. The notion of temporal divine punishment is central to this scheme. Since wickedness is always punished by God and suffering is the form that punishment takes, then Job's suffering must be the punishment of God. It follows that Job has committed wickedness. His suffering, therefore, is just. All his vain protestations of moral integrity are not merely self-delusion on his part, but the very height of blasphemy against God. If Job will only admit his guilt and passively submit, perhaps God will stay his hand and be merciful in his judgment. So, in the name of theological correctness, they plead with Job to accept his lot.

Job is familiar with such arguments. He does not deny that he is a sinner like all other human beings, but he cannot detect a sin in his life which merits such enormous suffering. His friends' arguments, which are based on a particularly narrow concept of justice, only intensify his consciousness of innocence. His experience has brought into question the shallow theology of his day. In the midst of his confusion and pain, made worse by the accusations of blasphemy made by those to whom he turned for support, and feeling persecuted by the "hand of God" upon his life, Job struggles to hold together these twin convictions: that God is just and that he, Job, is innocent in his suffering. What the worldview of his society held to be self-contradictory propositions, Job embraces as true to his experience. But how is he to speak of God from the perspective of his suffering?

As the book unfolds, we find the arguments of Job's friends becoming more repetitious and monotonous, while, in contrast, Job's perspective is enlarged. The first enlargement arises through Job's solidarity with all who suffer unjustly. His own suffering makes him sensitive to the plight of the poor. In a moving passage, reminiscent of the prophetic literature of the Old Testament, Job describes the concrete suffering of the poor – a suffering not decreed by destiny or due to inexplicable causes, but clearly the result of human wickedness:

> There are those who move boundary stones;
> they pasture flocks they have stolen.
> They drive away the orphan's donkey
> and take the widow's ox in pledge.
> They thrust the needy from the path
> and force all the poor of the land into hiding.
> Like wild donkeys in the desert
> the poor go about their labour of foraging food;
> the wasteland provides food for their children . . .
> The groans of the dying rise from the city,
> and the souls of the wounded cry out for help.
> But God charges no one with wrongdoing.
> (24:2–5, 12)

Job has launched a devastating attack on the "windy arguments" of his friends. He dismisses the latter as "miserable comforters" and "worthless physicians" (16:2; 13:4). Their self-assured theology does not bear on the real world of human suffering, hopes and fears. They think they are being faithful to God by passing on the tradition of "what the wise have declared, hiding nothing received from their ancestors" (15:18), namely, that the wicked live tormented lives and the upright are rewarded with happiness and prosperity. But this glib, abstract way of theologizing is the real blasphemy: they veil and distort the face of God. Seeking to justify God they only condemn innocent men and women. Job confronts them with the telling question: "Do you mean to defend God by prevarication and by dishonest argument?" (13:7, my paraphrase).

Job's rebelliousness is directed not primarily at the fact of his suffering but at the religious worldview that seeks to justify it. The God whom he is groping after in his turmoil is a God who both listens and speaks to humanity. Job boldly demands that God confront him with the charges against him, and this demand is inspired by a firm trust in the ultimate righteousness of God. Job is sure that God knows him to be innocent and will declare that to his friends. We, the readers of the book, know that Job is innocent and that God has declared him to be so, for the narrator has disclosed this to us in the prologue. But for Job the conviction that God alone knows the true situation is a conviction born of a living faith. He sees his struggle with God as a kind of lawsuit that he is bringing against God on behalf of wretched humanity. But through his tears he glimpses the presence of an advocate before the throne of God who will take up his case. Addressing the earth, which will receive the life that is now slipping away from him, he expresses his deepest hope in these words:

> Earth, do not cover my blood;
> may my cry never be laid to rest!
> Even now my witness is in heaven;
> my advocate is on high.
> My intercessor is my friend
> as my eyes pour out tears to God;
> on behalf of a man he pleads with God
> as one pleads for a friend.
> (16:18–21)

This mysterious mediator, an approachable friend before the awesome face of God, appears again in a passage that marks the high point of Job's spiritual pilgrimage:

> I know that my redeemer lives,
> and that in the end he will stand on the earth.
> And after my skin has been destroyed,
> yet in my flesh I will see God.
> (19:25–26)

Here Job refers to his *go'el*, his defender or avenger. The word arose out of the Israelites' sense of family solidarity, and it combined the thought of ransom with that of obligation. When someone fell into debt or suffered any misfortune, it was the obligation of the nearest relative to intervene. The law in Israel recognized the right of the *go'el*, the nearest relative, to redeem the property, freedom and life of those who were in no position to help themselves (e.g. Lev 25:47–49; Num 35:18–19). The term came to be used of Yahweh in his relationship with Israel as a whole. As a result of the covenant, God has become the nearest relative, the one who takes upon himself liability for his people, the one who rescues them and avenges them (e.g. Isa 43:14; 44:24; Prov 23:10–11).

To whom is Job appealing? Much scholarly ink has been spilt in answering this question. I myself have no hesitation in saying that Job is referring to God and not to an intermediary distinct from God. In an earlier passage he has already appealed to God to protect him from God's wrath (14:13); and now he glimpses a profound insight – that the God he experiences as his adversary is at the same time his truest friend. God is both his judge and the one who will defend him on the day of judgment. The One who wounds him is also his healer. God will not let him be destroyed "in the end" but rather "I myself will see him" (19:27) – not as a stranger or as an enemy, but in a friendship closer than the superficial friendships he now experiences. It is this hope that causes his heart to burst with moments of joy in the midst of his trials.

This dialectical approach to God is one of the most profound aspects of the book of Job, and the Christian reader can sense here an anguished but courageous "groping" towards the great themes of New Testament faith, especially the redemptive work of the cross and a "social" conception of the being of God. It reveals how the process of lament, while questioning theological "givens," can at the same time lead to new insights into one's relationship with God. This is made possible by refusing to be silenced by one's pain; the remarkable thing about Job is how he keeps on talking with God even though he must have felt that his communication was all one-way!

The justice of God has been the main subject of the arguments set forth by Job's companions. They equate divine justice with retributive punishment. God gives to individuals according to their deserts. The outworking of divine government is, in their minds, crystal clear. In this perspective Job's sufferings are the result of his guilt. Job, on the other hand, begins not with theological principles but with his own experience. He declares his innocence and integrity.

But what Job's companions cannot grasp (and what contemporary readers also fail to recognize) is that Job's quest is not an intellectual one. He is faced with an existential and relational crisis, not a theological problem ("the problem of evil"). His familiar world, the moral order in creation he has taken for granted, has collapsed. Why has God, his lifelong protector, now become his enemy? It is God's credibility, his dependability in Job's eyes, that is now at stake. And troubled by this question, which is utterly blasphemous to his friends, Job demands a personal response from God:

> But I desire to speak to the Almighty
> and to argue my case with God.
> You, however, smear me with lies;
> you are worthless physicians, all of you!
> (13:3–4)

Job's Vindication

Job is granted his request. God answers him from "out of the storm" (38:1). This is a classic image in the Bible, forming the context for a *theophany* – a physical disclosure of God's presence. The storm both conveys and conceals the fearsome majesty of God. And for the first time since the prologue to the book the author uses the covenant name of Yahweh in speaking of God. God is no longer distant and detached, but the gracious and faithful Lord of the covenant. He has been present all along, but now that presence is made known to Job.

At first sight there is something unsatisfying, indeed disconcerting, about the divine speech. Yahweh does not rebuke Job for any sin (thus confirming his innocence) but neither does he answer the anguished questions that Job has fired at the heavens. He adopts the same confrontational posture that Job has assumed in his lawsuit against God, even appearing like a cosmic bully: "Brace yourself like a man; I will question you, and you shall answer me" (38:3). There is no apology for God's long silence, no word of consolation for Job in his distress. But nor does God crush and humiliate him. He takes him instead on a whirlwind tour of the universe, educating him about stars and animals and monstrous creatures of the deep, in poetry that ranks amongst the most beautiful and evocative in world literature. But, however bewildered the reader may be, Job understands (see 40:3–4 and 42:1–6).

Relatively few interpreters of the book of Job seek to share Job's understanding. They assume that what God says is less important than the fact of God's speaking, the communication of God's presence to Job. Consequently, they pay little attention to the content of the divine speech. In their view, the very presence of God is sufficient to satisfy the deepest desires of Job. While acknowledging the truth in this, I believe it to be deficient. Instead I endorse the view of Gustavo Gutiérrez that the "content[s] of God's speeches specify and concretize the response; the word of God gives the presence of God its full meaning."[8]

There are several themes which run through the two divine speeches (38:1 – 40:2 and 40:6 – 41:34), but prominent among them are the following:

(a) The Gratuitousness of Divine Love

At the very beginning of the speech, Yahweh directs Job's attention to the very source of all existing things. The universe in all its wonder and mystery does not turn around Job or any other human being. The majesty of God is to be identified less with might than with creative freedom and the gratuitous initiative of love. It is this that enfolds the creation and gives meaning to God's work, whether in nature or history.

> Where were you when I laid the earth's foundation?
> Tell me, if you understand.
> Who marked off its dimensions? Surely you know!
> Who stretched a measuring line across it?
> On what were its footings set,
> or who laid its cornerstone –
> while the morning stars sang together
> and all the angels shouted for joy?
> (38:4–7)

The teasing irony of God's speech exposes the limitations of human perspectives. We are not the centre of reality. And the doctrine of retribution, though it has a legitimate place in God's government of things, is not the key to understanding the universe. The free and gratuitous love of God is the hinge on which the universe turns. The world expresses the freedom and delight of God in creating. Utility is not the reason behind creation: not everything that exists was made to be useful to human beings, and therefore their true meaning can never be fathomed within an anthropocentric worldview.

> Who cuts a channel for the torrents of rain,
> and a path for the thunderstorm,
> to water a land where no one lives,
> an uninhabited desert,

8. Gustavo Gutiérrez, *On Job: God-Talk and the Suffering of the Innocent*, English trans. (Maryknoll, NY: Orbis, 1987), 69.

to satisfy a desolate wasteland
and make it sprout with grass?
(38:25–27)

What purpose does rain serve in places empty of human dwelling? Can Job and his friends celebrate with Yahweh the wonder and beauty of creation – without expecting that Yahweh's actions in the world of nature and history fit the predictive schemes of human reason? On what basis do they claim to know how God is going to act? What do you make of God's joke – the ostrich (39:13): a creature bereft of good sense, flapping her wings but getting nowhere, leaving her eggs in the earth unaware that someone may step on them (39:15)! Even those parts of creation which seem lacking in wisdom and purpose have their place in God's ordering of things. Perhaps the ostrich is a picture of Job himself – a paradoxical mixture of greatness and foolishness. They are both endowed with value by the gratuitous love of God.

David Atkinson discovers here a simple but profound pastoral application:

> God, we are told in Genesis, made the man and put him in a garden that was "pleasant to the sight." The context in which we live our lives contributes significantly to our sense of well-being. The ash heap may be an appropriate place on which to sit if we are in mourning, but it is no place to stay if we wish to feel better. Sometimes we will most help distressed people – help them draw nearer to God, from the depths of depression – not by teaching them doctrine, or by preaching our best sermon, or by showing them the error of their ways, but by walking with them around the garden, by taking them to see a waterfall or a sunset, by helping them recover an enjoyment in the world. Such steps are not always practicable, of course. But in so far as we can enable depressed people to see themselves in a new setting, and to recover a place of security and belonging within the rich panorama of God's creation, we are helping them. They need to know that they, too, *belong*. It is by enjoying the Creator's handiwork that we often begin to feel again the touch of the Creator's hand.[9]

I began this chapter with George Steiner's passionate and depressing reminder of the pervasiveness of evil in human life, down the centuries no less than in the present age. But that perspective needs to be placed alongside another, equally realistic, about our human situation. The Harvard developmental

9. David Atkinson, *The Message of Job* (Leicester: Inter-Varsity Press, 1991), 147.

psychologist Jerome Kagan reminds us that "What is biologically special about our species is a constant attention to what is good and beautiful and a dislike of all that is bad and ugly." Kagan is not a Christian, but what he reminds us of is what is theologically understood as either God's "common grace" or that our humanity still retains "the image of God" despite its propensity to evil. "The number of acts of rudeness, vandalism, theft, abuse, rape, and murder that occurred yesterday, throughout the world, is infinitesimal when compared with the total number of opportunities each adult had to display these behaviours. The ratio of asocial acts to total opportunities approaches zero every day."[10]

(b) The Sovereignty of Divine Wisdom

God has intimated to Job that there is indeed a divine plan unfolding in all of creation, but it is not one that the human mind can grasp so as to draw straightforward cause-and-effect patterns. But this should not be surprising when there is so much in God's world that eludes human control. If the creation cannot be domesticated, how presumptuous to think that the Creator's actions can!

> Who shut up the sea behind doors
>   when it burst forth from the womb,
> when I made the clouds its garment
>   and wrapped it in thick darkness,
> when I fixed limits for it
>   and set its doors and bars in place,
> when I said, "This far you may come and no farther;
>   here is where your proud waves halt"?
> (38:8–11)

The sea is a common biblical symbol of chaos, social and physical, restless and uncontrollable, its proud waves threatening to engulf the land and its inhabitants. But God has set limits to it; its fearsome power is subject to God's power. Likewise the monstrous, mysterious sea creatures Behemoth and Leviathan, which make their appearance in the second divine speech, probably represent the terrifying forces of chaos and disorder that seek to overpower human life and the rest of creation. Powerful though they be, they are themselves held within the more powerful hand of the Creator. From the perspective of his suffering Job sees the creation as a chaos, a return to

---

10. Jerome Kagan, *Three Seductive Ideas* (Cambridge, MA: Harvard University Press, 1998), 191–192.

emptiness. Disorder and meaninglessness seem to have triumphed. God shows him that the divine power controls these chaotic powers even though they are not annihilated. There is evil in the world, but the world itself is not evil. There is chaos in the cosmos, but the cosmos is not a chaos. No power on earth, however hideous and terrifying in its aspect, can separate us from the Creator's embrace.

> Who has a claim against me that I must pay?
> Everything under heaven belongs to me.
> (41:11)

(c) The Patience of Divine Justice

As the broadside of ironic questioning continues, God invites Job to contemplate what he would do if he were in God's place!

> Have you ever given orders to the morning,
> or shown the dawn its place,
> that it might take the earth by the edges
> and shake the wicked out of it?
> (38:12–13)

Job has accused God of turning a blind eye to the atrocities committed by the wicked (21:7, 29–31; 24:12). To "shake the wicked out" of the earth is what he has been demanding of God. But God's light continues to dawn on them. Is the moral order of creation therefore flawed? All right, says God, you take over the running of the universe.

> Would you discredit my justice?
> Would you condemn me to justify yourself? . . .
> Unleash the fury of your wrath,
> look at all who are proud and bring them low,
> look at all who are proud and humble them,
> crush the wicked where they stand.
> Bury them all in the dust together;
> shroud their faces in the grave.
> Then I myself will admit to you
> that your own right hand can save you.
> (40:8, 11–14)

The irony employed in this passage brings home to Job the self-imposed limitations of the divine love. Insignificant though human beings may seem to Job, they are precious enough in Yahweh's eyes for Yahweh to heed their freedom, to bear with patience their wickedness and to seek their collaboration in the just government of the world. The divine freedom that Yahweh has revealed to Job has its correlate in human freedom. The latter is established by, and grounded in, the first. Grace involves the communion of these two freedoms. Job's freedom found expression in his vehement complaints at God. God's freedom finds expression in the shocking generosity of grace that refuses to be confined within a system of predictable rewards and punishments. Until that terrible day of final reckoning, when evil and evildoers will be eradicated and all suffering innocents vindicated, Yahweh indicates that he does not take pleasure in the death of the wicked but wills that they turn from their wickedness to life (see e.g. Ezek 18:23; Mic 7:18; Hos 11:8–9; 1 Tim 2:3–4; 2 Pet 3:9).

Job has travelled a long and tortuous road to his personal encounter with Yahweh. The answers he has got are not what he was looking for, but he has been liberated from his anxieties and found his hope fulfilled. That Job understands and is transformed by Yahweh's speeches is shown by his response:

> I know that you can do all things;
> no purpose of yours can be thwarted . . .
> My ears had heard of you
> but now my eyes have seen you.
> Therefore I despise myself
> and repent in dust and ashes.
> (42:2, 5–6)

God does have plans for his world, and that world is not a chaos as Job had repeatedly suggested in his dispute with his friends. His reasoning had then seemed to be: "I do not understand these plans. Therefore, they cannot exist." But the integrity of his faith, expressed in his willingness to confront the contradiction between experience and a doctrine of temporal retribution, and to plead the issue not only with his friends but with God himself, has led to another way of perceiving and speaking about God. As Gutiérrez finely puts it, "What he has now heard from the mouth of Yahweh has given him a glimpse of another world, an order different from the one he rejected but for which until now there seemed to be no alternative. All this is still not entirely clear to him, but at least he is no longer being suffocated by the religious universe of his friends and indeed of his age."[11]

11. Gutiérrez, *On Job*, 84.

What is the repentance that Job performs? Gutiérrez points out, following other commentators, that the verbs in the last line have no object. NIV's "despise myself" is misleading; the New Jerusalem Bible is closer to the mark in translating it as "I retract." But we still face the question: what does Job retract? Yahweh has not accused him of any sin, and indeed Yahweh goes on to declare that Job alone has spoken correctly about him (42:7–9). The verb *nahum* (translated here "repent") usually means "to change one's mind," "to abandon an opinion" (see e.g. Exod 32:12, 14; Jer 18:8, 10; Amos 7:3, 6). The image of "dust and ashes" describes the situation of Job before the dialogues began, one of humiliation and lamentation. If we follow Gutiérrez in taking this to be the object of both verbs in the sentence, we can then translate Job's response to mean: "I repudiate and abandon dust and ashes."

This way of translating makes Job's response both coherent and consistent with Yahweh's verdict about his servant. Job is expressing not contrition as much as a decisive rejection of the attitude of dejection that had been his until now. Job has now surrendered to love, a love that met him in the heart of the storm. His trust has been renewed, his horizons expanded; he now truly believes "for nothing."

(d) The Particularity of Divine Engagement

Yahweh's final words are a rebuke of the speeches of Job's friends. "[Yahweh] said to Eliphaz the Temanite, 'I am angry with you and your two friends, because you have not spoken the truth about me, as my servant Job has'" (42:7). What is strange, though, is that the friends' arguments were reflections of the covenantal theology of the book of Deuteronomy and much of the wisdom literature: God, in his justice, rewards the righteous and judges the wicked. How can Job's rebellious speech be "right" and the "orthodoxy" of his friends be wrong?

Following Gutiérrez, I believe that Yahweh's words point to a failure in much modern Western theology. When the latter is cut off from the lived experience of people, especially their experience of personal suffering and dying, it becomes hollow. No universal theological system can deal adequately with the particularities of human experience. We need the nuanced, "polyphonic" approach of David Fergusson, mentioned above, if we are to include experiences that go against the grain of our received theological framework. Job's friends have failed to properly "contextualize" their theology. Gutiérrez writes: "The language we use depends on the situation we are in. Job's words are a criticism of every theology that lacks human compassion and contact with reality; the one-directional movement from theological principles to life really goes nowhere."[12]

Scott Ellington develops this thought further. He agrees with those scholars that the great majority of ways the prepositional phrase *elay* used in 42:7c is translated in the Old Testament is not as "of me" or "about me" but, rather, "to me." Indeed, in the very next verse, Yahweh tells Eliphaz that Job his servant will "pray for you." The problem with Job's friends, then, is that all their speech was *about* God and not *to* God, as Job's was. Job's friends are not engaged in dialogue, as Job is with God, because they have all the "right answers" and are not open to the possibility of being corrected. Content alone, divorced from both context and relationality, does not constitute truthful speech. "This raises the intriguing possibility that *right speech* may, in certain contexts, include *wrong content* from a theological perspective."[13]

I am reminded of the idiosyncratic philosopher Søren Kierkegaard, whose sharp criticisms of the "Christendom theology" of his society (nineteenth-century Denmark) are still pertinent today, not least in his own country. In one of his journal entries, Kierkegaard wrote: "The moment I take Christianity as a doctrine and so indulge my cleverness or profundity or my eloquence or my imaginative powers in depicting it: people are very pleased, and I am looked upon as a serious Christian. The moment I begin to express existentially what I say, and consequently to bring Christianity into reality: it is just as though I had exploded existence – the scandal is there at once."[14]

Clifford Williams observes that to make his point, Kierkegaard often exaggerated.

> He declared that "truth is subjectivity" and that one could be "in the truth" even if one were passionately connected to what is objectively false. He said that faith has nothing to do with knowledge. He exaggerated because he thought that those who believed they were rightly connected to God because of their beliefs about God were blinded by those beliefs. He thought, in fact, that they were trying to evade God by having the beliefs. More accurately, the true source of the evasion was having the same beliefs as everyone else in nineteenth-century Denmark. It was merely a "crowd faith," not a genuine connection to God.

12. Gutiérrez, 30.

13. Ellington, *Risking Truth*, 118.

14. Søren Kierkegaard, *Journals of Søren Kierkegaard: A Selection*, ed. and trans. A. Dru (London: Fontana, 1958), 174.

> Kierkegaard gets at the connection between having a crowd faith and evasion: "The most pernicious of all evasions is – hidden in the crowd, to want, as it were, to avoid God's inspection of oneself as a single individual, avoid hearing God's voice as a single individual."[15]

A Humble Empathy

The sceptical, anti-theistic arguments of today's prominent media atheists are easily rebutted by intelligent Christians. But why do we, at the same time, find Western Christian books on apologetics, especially those coming out of American evangelical circles, so unsatisfying? Because they exude a rationalistic and triumphalist temper: everything is cut and dried, there are no loose threads, nothing in the other's position that may be a serious challenge to faith. Moreover, the apologist's own way of life is deemed wholly irrelevant to the theological positions he or she adopts and the arguments he or she advances.

The questions that the Hebrew prophets, Job and the psalmists raise are often more ruthless than those of today's sceptics. Doubt and dispute, both about God and with God, have always been part of the Jewish and Christian worlds; and there is a long tradition of Christian wrestling with God in prayer that has given rise to some of the greatest Christian theological works.[16] "The preacher must dip his pen into the blood of his heart; then he can also reach the ear of his neighbour" was the advice given by Gregory the Great (540–604 CE) to those monks who were sent to evangelize Europe.[17] And the words of Martin Luther (1483–1546 CE) are salutary for all theologians and theological students today: "I did not learn my theology all at once, but I had to search deeper for it, where my trials and temptations took me . . . living, nay rather dying and being damned make a theologian, not understanding, reading or speculation."[18]

---

15. Clifford Williams, *Existential Reasons for Belief in God: A Defense of Desires and Emotions for Faith* (Downers Grove, IL: IVP Academic, 2011), 172–173.

16. St Augustine's *Confessions* and St Anselm's *Cur Deus Homo?*, both theological classics, are extended prayers to God. A more recent example is Karl Rahner, *Encounters with Silence* (Westminster, MD: Newman Press, 1965).

17. Gregory the Great, *Homilies on Ezekiel*, quoted in Pope Benedict XVI, *Great Christian Thinkers: From the Early Church through the Middle Ages* (London: SPCK, 2011), 145.

18. Martin Luther, *Autobiographical Preface* (1545), cited in Gordon Rupp, *The Righteousness of God* (London: Hodder & Stoughton, 1953), 102.

It is this lack of empathy with those who suffer that makes so much apologetics and Christian preaching appear "unreal" and rings hollow in the ears of those who suffer. The Nigerian novelist Ben Okri, speaking about the death of his mother, tells his interviewer about his disappointment with the church:

> The reason is because at the time, I experienced something very peculiar. I realised that the pastor, the priest who was speaking to me at the time about my grief, spoke to me from the book but not from the experience, so he could not speak to the grief in me. He couldn't speak to the emptiness in me because, at the time, he hadn't gone through it himself. I can say this now with a certain amount of tranquillity, because about four years later his mother died and he wrote to me and said, "Oh my goodness. I didn't know. That's what you were going through at the time."[19]

---

19. Ben Okri, in Bel Mooney, *Devout Sceptics: Conversations on Faith and Doubt* (London: Hodder & Stoughton, 2004), 97.

3

The Tears of God

> It is not some religious act which makes a Christian what he is, but participation in the suffering of God in the life of the world.[1]

We have seen that lament is born at the point of collision between faith and experience, belief and expectation. Of course, these categories are not rigid, watertight binaries. Our everyday beliefs are formed through experience, especially in early childhood, and shaped by life within the institutions of family, school, church, temple or mosque, and mass media. Our expectations depend on and reflect those beliefs. And experience does not come to us "raw" but cooked through a cultural and social framework.

Even pain, which is often regarded as the "rawest," most private and thought-independent of experiences, is nothing of the sort. The notorious phenomenon of phantom limb pain and the way distress and sickness can be caused by anger or repressed memories show that pain is not only experienced in but also generated by the mind and socially anchored. Pain inflicted as a form of punishment is experienced differently depending on whether it is understood as deserving or as purely arbitrary. The pains of childbirth or religious martyrdom are framed within narratives of "normality" and "hope." Humans are social beings and, as the social anthropologist Talal Asad reminds us, "their suffering is partly constituted by the way they inhabit, or are constrained to inhabit, their relationship with others. Pain is not always an insufferable agony or a chronic condition . . . But as a social relationship

1. Dietrich Bonhoeffer, *Letters and Papers from Prison*, English trans. (London: SCM, 1953; London: Collins, 1959), Letter of 18 July 1944, 123.

pain is more than an experience. It is part of what creates the conditions of action and experience."[2]

The great St Augustine (354–430 CE) scornfully dismissed as superstition the stories of miracles told him with awe by his fellow Christians. He believed, of course, in the biblical miracles, but held to the view that these had ceased with the death of the apostles. Later in life, having served as Bishop of Hippo, he changed his mind, offering prayers for the sick and even compiling a list of contemporary miracles. What changed his mind was not deeper study of the Bible or new philosophical ideas, but simply coming into pastoral contact with the everyday lives and concerns of ordinary Christians in his city. Where he once saw only ignorance and superstition, he now saw the love and power of God.[3]

New experiences, whether like Augustine's or of pain and loss or cross-cultural encounters, will always unsettle our beliefs. We normally attempt to interpret these new experiences by seeking to expand rather than radically dismantle our deeply held beliefs. We can also insulate our beliefs from such disturbances by refusing to grant our experiences any epistemic status. This is how political and religious cults retain their hold on their believers: all stories about the immoralities or inconsistencies of their leaders are dismissed as "enemy propaganda." Or, if we are brought up to believe that God will heal us of any and every sickness, then lack of healing can be attributed to a lack of faith or a moral failing on one's part. But, as the instances of such dissonance between belief and experience continue to mount, it creates an enormous emotional strain. We either reject our belief system outright and convert to another. Or we could explore what might be weak, one-sided or erroneous in our beliefs and seek to renew and reform them in the light of our changing experience.

This latter option is what enables Christian theological development. The twentieth-century experiences of environmental degradation, the massive loss of biodiversity and global warming resulting in severe climatic change forced serious readers of the Bible to discover large swathes of text that were routinely ignored in traditional churches: texts that spoke of God's delight in the non-human creation and the responsibility of humans to care for the earth and all its creatures. Similarly, the experiences of women in patriarchal

---

2. Talal Asad, "Thinking about Agency and Pain," in *Formations of the Secular: Christianity, Islam, Modernity* (Stanford, CA: Stanford University Press, 2003), 84.

3. Peter Brown, *Augustine of Hippo: A Biography* (Berkeley, CA: University of California Press, 1967), 413–418.

societies and churches have forced a rethinking of the theologies and traditional interpretations of biblical texts that have, wittingly or unwittingly, justified such patriarchal oppression. And a plethora of postmodern and postcolonial theologies have sought to liberate Christianity from its associations with racism, global capitalism and ideologies of empire.

The Prophets and Divine Suffering[4]

In the aftermath of the atomic bombings of Hiroshima and Nagasaki, and the carnage of the Second World War, the Japanese theologian Kazoh Kitamori wrote a much-discussed book called *Theology of the Pain of God.* Kitamori saw his time as an age of "death and pain." He explained that "in every period of history, life and death, joy and pain are intertwined. In some periods, life and joy are more pronounced than death and pain . . . There are also periods when death and pain are more pronounced than life and joy."[5] In such an age, "The heart of the gospel was revealed to me as 'the pain of God.'"[6] This pain was the tension within the being of God between his love for humanity and his just desire to punish human sin. "An absolute being without wrath can have no real pain," he writes. "The pain of God is his love – this love is based on the premise of his wrath, which is absolute, inflexible reality."[7] Kitamori distinguishes this "transcendent pain" in God from his "immanent pain" in sharing the suffering of his creatures, but has little to say about the latter. Indeed, he drives too sharp a wedge between the two. The "transcendent pain" of God is something that happens within the being of God – he writes that "the pain of God is part of his essence . . . The Bible reveals that the pain of God belongs to his eternal being."[8]

Despite some unsatisfactory aspects, Kitamori's bold and challenging emphasis on the "pain of God" plants him within a growing line of twentieth-century theologians who have directly challenged the classical Christian teaching that while God suffers in the humanity of his incarnate Son, Jesus

4. I have benefited greatly in what follows from Terence E. Fretheim, *The Suffering of God: An Old Testament Perspective* (Philadelphia: Fortress, 1984); Scott A. Ellington, *Risking Truth: Reshaping the World through Prayers of Lament* (Eugene, OR: Pickwick, 2008); and Paul Fiddes, *The Creative Suffering of God* (Oxford: Clarendon Press, 1988).

5. Kazoh Kitamori, *Theology of the Pain of God*, trans. M. E. Bratcher (London: SCM, 1966), 136.

6. Kitamori, *Theology of the Pain of God*, 19.

7. Kitamori, 27.

8. Kitamori, 45.

Christ, God himself remains *impassible*, untouched and unaffected by his relationship with his creation.[9] The horrors of the Second World War, especially the Shoah and the atom bombings, was a spur to the rejection of this tradition by many European thinkers. For instance, Dietrich Bonhoeffer, in a famous letter of 16 July 1944 from his Nazi prison, stated that

> Before God and with him we live without God. God allows himself to be edged out of the world and on to the cross. God is weak and powerless in the world, and that is exactly the way, the only way, in which he can be with us and help us . . . This is the decisive difference between Christianity and all religions. Man's religiosity makes him look in his distress to the power of God in the world; he uses God as a *Deus ex machina*. The Bible however directs him to the powerlessness and suffering of God; only a suffering God can help.[10]

It is important to note that Bonhoeffer did not speak of a helpless and absent God, but of a God who rejects what the world calls power (which the church has so often embraced) and chooses instead to work through solidarity with human weakness and suffering. Bonhoeffer has been speaking of the overthrow by the world of a "false conception of God" which has now "cleared the decks" for the "God of the Bible who conquers power and space in the world by his weakness."[11]

The "false conception of God" embodied in classical Christian theism, from its early years, was influenced by Greek philosophical ideas of perfection. For Plato, if God is the perfect, timeless, self-sufficient Supreme Good, he must be changeless, for change can only be to a state that is inferior to what he already is. He cannot be dependent on another, for that would imply imperfection. He cannot be affected by what other beings do, let alone experience suffering, for that would imply change. Aristotle, too, envisaged God as the First Cause, the Unmoved Mover, who eternally contemplates his own thoughts as that is the highest perfection. Some of the classical theologians of the early church, influenced as they were by this prevailing philosophical climate, tended to read

---

9. Paul Fiddes proposes four reasons for the remarkable (but not universal) theological reversal of traditional notions of divine immutability and impassibility: (1) reflections on God's love in the light of modern psychological understandings of personal relationships; (2) the recovery of the centrality of the cross of Christ; (3) the magnitude of human suffering; and (4) the world picture of cosmic and human evolution. See chapter 1 of Fiddes, *Creative Suffering*.

10. Bonhoeffer, *Letters and Papers*, 122.

11. Bonhoeffer, 122.

into biblical teaching of God's constancy and faithfulness these metaphysical notions of unchanging, timeless Being; and God's moral and ontological otherness (his holiness) to his creation tended towards a philosophical distancing from the messiness of the world and all the suffering of history. Yes, God suffered in the incarnation of the Word in the human nature of Christ, but the Word itself was immune to suffering.[12]

The classical theologians tended to understand love as an attitude and action that aims at the *good* of another, and not a matter of feelings. "His pity is not the wretched heart of a fellow-sufferer," wrote Augustine of the perfect love of God; "the pity of God is the goodness of his help . . . when God pities, he does not grieve and he liberates."[13] He effects relief for us, while not being affected in his feelings by our suffering. In seeking to avoid our idolatrous tendency to project our states of mind onto God and so think of God as simply a superhuman being, many of the classical theologians went too far in distancing God's being from his creation.

From the opening chapters of the Bible, we encounter a God who is *in relationship* with his creation. God is not a passionless chess master moving pieces around a board or unilaterally directing a drama in accordance with a preordained script. In bringing a creation into being, the Triune God opens God's inner life to an "other"; he makes himself vulnerable in an act of self-giving love. God has freely chosen to be God in relationship with us. And a relationship with creatures who have abused their freedom and resist God's loving purposes for them entails pain and suffering in the heart of God.

---

12. Tertullian (155–220 CE)'s treatise *Against Praxeas*, ch. 29, is often claimed to be the first clear statement of the doctrine. No doubt Tertullian believes it, but his primary concern here, at an early stage of Trinitarian development, is to refute the identification of Christ with God the Father and so to assert that the Father died, as accursed for us. Therefore, the claim may be exaggerated. Also, there is little trace of Greek philosophical influence on him, unlike in later thinkers (http://www.tertullian.org/articles/evans_praxeas_eng.htm). See J. N. D. Kelly, *Early Christian Doctrines*, 5th ed. (1958; London: A&C Black, 1977), 299 (on Gregory of Nyssa) and 322 (on Cyril of Alexandria). Typical of the tradition would be this comment by Anselm: "Therefore when we state that God undergoes some lowliness or weakness, we understand this to be in accordance with the weakness of the human substance which he assumed [in incarnation], not in accordance with the sublimity of his impassible [divine] nature." Anselm, "Cur Deus Homo?," in *Anselm of Canterbury*, ed. and trans. Jasper Hopkins and Herbert Richardson, 4 vols. (New York: Edwin Mellen Press, 1976), 3:58–59.

13. Cited in Paul Fiddes, *Creative Suffering*, 17. Rare exceptions are found in the "mystical" tradition, beginning with the mysterious author of the late fifth century who wrote under the pseudonym Dionysius the Areopagite. The latter boldly spoke of God's "ecstatic" *desire* (Gk *eros*) for his creation, to which our human desires are a response. See Andrew Louth, *Denys the Areopagite* (London: Geoffrey Chapman, 1989), 95. But even here, the implications for God of his desire being frustrated by human sin are not explored.

We saw this, in the opening chapter, in regard to Genesis 6:5–6. God's "grief" and "change of heart" over the wickedness of humanity has been taken as anthropomorphic language by most biblical readers. Of course, all biblical language about God is metaphorical and analogical.[14] When we use terms like "exist" or "love" or "wrath" or "Father" or "Judge" in relation to God, we draw similarities with our customary human use of these terms but also recognize their difference. God does not "exist" in the way we creatures exist (namely, in space–time and dependent on the Creator and other creatures). God's "wrath" is not fitful, fickle and subject to the vagaries of human prejudice; rather, it is a constant and consistent opposition to evil. Metaphorical references to God drawn from the world of human relations (anthropomorphisms) share this ambivalence. God does not repent like humans (1 Sam 15:29), but he is free to change direction within his unwavering and ultimate intention to reconcile his broken creation, liberating it from its bondage to sin and death. God engages with us temporally, though his relationship with the world also transcends time. He not only initiates but also *responds* to the free decisions of humans. It is in the context of that covenantal faithfulness, both to his creation and to ancient Israel, that God's grief and his anger are to be understood.

Terence Fretheim notes that anthropomorphic metaphors predominate in Israelite talk about God and are a point of distinctiveness when read against the backdrop of the religious world of the ancient Near East (cf. the use of animal–human hybrids). He goes on to point out that it is also ironic that Christians should have trouble with this language. For "In the incarnation, God has acted anthropomorphically in the most supreme way. The New Testament, far from being the culmination of a progressive spiritualization of the understanding of God, speaks of God unsurpassably enfleshed in the human. Apart from the Christ-event, the New Testament continues to speak of God in terms of such metaphors."[15] Because the Triune God is among us, closer to us than we are

14. Janet Martin Soskice suggests as a working definition of metaphor, "that figure of speech whereby we speak about one thing in terms which are seen to be suggestive of another." *Metaphor and Religious Language* (1985; Oxford: Clarendon, 1987), 15. The two things brought into conjunction with each other are usually from two different realms, and their differences are as important as the similarities.

15. Fretheim, *Suffering of God*, 6–7. Indeed, the theme of the "humanity of God" has been the burden of some of the great twentieth-century theologians such as Karl Barth and Eberhard Jüngel. The latter proposed, on the basis of the coming of God to humanity in Jesus, an "analogy of advent" in the use of theological language: "There is Christological reason to ask whether there is not a God-enabled, a God-required, even a God-demanded anthropomorphism." Eberhard Jüngel, *God As the Mystery of the World*, trans. D. L. Guder (Edinburgh: T&T Clark, 1983), 280.

to ourselves, similar in dissimilarity, there is a proper way to think and speak of God in human terms.

The words of Genesis 6:5–6 indicate that God is affected by what goes on in the world.[16] The flood story that follows and the covenant with Noah reveals his self-limitation in exercising power: God will continue to be involved with his rebellious image on earth (humanity) and will not abandon them to their folly. This entails suffering for God, in addition to the suffering unleashed by humans on their fellow humans and the earth. Two other Old Testament texts which use the language of divine "grieving" are Psalm 78:40–41 and Isaiah 63:7–10. This is God's response to human sin, along with compassion (Ps 78:38) and anger (78:21, 31); and it is not limited to the Old Testament, as Paul's injunction to the Ephesians in Ephesians 4:30 indicates. God's history of grieving continues.[17]

Furthermore, God does not "need" the world in the sense that there is some deficiency in his nature that the world meets; but he does need the world in the sense that he has *humbly and freely chosen* to be in a personal (that is, mutually responsive) relationship with his world. And God, in choosing to suffer out of his commitment to a wayward humanity, is not incapacitated or overwhelmed by this experience of suffering, nor does it embitter him so that he lashes out in vengeance. Even on those occasions when God employs human acts of violence and war in judgment on Israel and other nations, we can agree with Stephen Williams that

16. The language is hyperbolic. The narrator obviously did not envisage a world in which no kind souls nor acts of goodness ever existed. The larger genre in which it is embedded is parabolic/mythical.

17. The influence of John Calvin is hard to resist. For Calvin, because of our weakness, God "accommodates" himself to our capacity in order that he may be understood, and any notion of "change" in God purely reflects a human standpoint: "Now the mode of accommodation is for him to represent himself to us not as he is in himself, but as he seems to us. Although he is beyond all disturbance of mind, yet he testifies that he is angry toward sinners. Therefore whenever we hear that God is angered, we ought not to imagine any emotion in him, but rather to consider that this expression has been taken from our own human experience . . . So we ought not to understand anything else under the word 'repentance' than change of action . . . meanwhile, neither God's plan nor his will is reversed, nor his volition altered; but what he had from eternity foreseen, approved, and decreed, he pursues in uninterrupted tenor, however sudden the variation may appear in men's eyes." John Calvin, *Institutes of the Christian Religion*, ed. John T. McNeill, 2 vols. (Philadelphia: Westminster, 1960), 1.17.13. However, all great thinkers reveal inconsistencies over their lifetimes. And Calvin is no exception. When, unlike in the *Institutes*, he wrestles with biblical texts themselves, he speaks of the pathos of God, his vulnerable love, and the wounds of the world being the wounds of God himself. It is not insignificant that Calvin suffered much, as an exile and refugee. See the illuminating article by Nicholas Wolterstorff, "Calvin and the Wounds of God," *Reformed Journal* 37, no. 6 (June 1987): 14–22.

> If and where God ever commands what he abhors, we may be sure that he does so with a heavy heart and as the alternative to wiping out evil and suffering at a stroke, on the one hand, and turning his back on it so that it follows its own godless course, on the other . . . If God commands violence, it is part of a whole concessionary scheme of operation, an accommodation to the fact of rampant evil which he detests but has not abolished.[18]

In a marriage relationship, two persons set out on a voyage of love and discovery. If we think analogously of God's creational relationship with human persons, he creates a covenant partner who is other than himself, and assumes the "risk of faith" as he journeys with that partner. Following Fretheim, we can understand the variety of Old Testament texts that deal with the suffering of God in a threefold manner. First, God suffers *because* of his people's rejection of his covenant and their turning to idolatry which only dehumanizes them; second, God suffers *with* people who are suffering; and, third, God suffers *for* his people.[19]

The Old Testament prophets enjoyed a relationship with Yahweh (the LORD) that was unique in Israel. They were Yahweh's spokespersons to the nation and, on occasion, to other neighbouring nations. They were called not only to preach but to *embody* their message in symbolic acts and indeed the whole of their lives. When this was a hard message, describing the people's injustices and idolatries which evoked divine condemnation, it entailed discomfort and intense pain. While God and his prophet remained distinct, the suffering of the prophet – either because of his own anguish over the burden of his message or because of the rejection he himself experienced at the hands of his compatriots – mirrored the suffering of God. Indeed, the prophetic call was to participate in the pathos of God.

A prophetic message begins "not with hellfire and damnation, but with a picture of the pain and anguish of God" (cf. Isa 1:2–3; Jer 2:2).[20] The laments of Yahweh's prophet, such as we find in Jeremiah, are evoked by the laments of Yahweh himself. The prophet personifies the suffering of God, so that it is not always clear when the prophetic laments have as their subject Jeremiah and when it is the voice of Yahweh that we hear. Jeremiah 12:7–13, 15:5–9 and 18:13–19 contain the laments of God embedded in the laments of his

---

18. Stephen N. Williams, in J. Gordon McConville and Stephen N. Williams, *Joshua* (Grand Rapids, MI: Eerdmans, 2010), 121.

19. Fretheim, *Suffering of God*, 108.

20. Fretheim, 115.

prophet. The most poignant lament shared by the prophet and God is found in Jeremiah 8:18 – 9:11:

> Since my people are crushed, I am crushed;
>   I mourn, and horror grips me.
> Is there no balm in Gilead?
>   Is there no physician there?
> Why then is there no healing
>   for the wound of my people?
> Oh, that my head were a spring of water
>   and my eyes a fountain of tears!
> I would weep day and night
>   for the slain of my people.
> Oh, that I had in the desert
>   a lodging place for travellers,
> so that I might leave my people
>   and go away from them;
> for they are all adulterers,
>   a crowd of unfaithful people.
> (8:21 – 9:2)

"Unlike Job," observes Ellington, "Jeremiah takes up the suffering of another. He finds himself abused and abandoned precisely because he accepted the calling to take up God's offence and weep with him. Jeremiah stands in a new place, heretofore only hinted at in the Psalter. The pain that brings a protest to Jeremiah's lips is the pain of God. It is this burden that shapes the prophetic lament."[21]

The tenderness of Yahweh's love for his covenant people is expressed in the well-known words of Hosea 11, and especially verse 8:

> How can I give you up, Ephraim?
>   How can I hand you over, Israel?
> How can I treat you like Admah?
>   How can I make you like Zeboyim?
> My heart is changed within me;
>   all my compassion is aroused.

Even as God's wrath expresses his justice, it is tempered with his tears.

---

21. Ellington, *Risking Truth*, 143.

Thus, divine judgment on the lips of the prophets is better conceived in terms of a breakdown in a marriage relationship caused by the unfaithfulness of a beloved spouse, rather than as the cold, impersonal sentencing of a courtroom judge. God expresses hurt and outrage as his trust is betrayed and all his overtures towards rapprochement are spurned continually.

> It is striking how commonly the language of God's judgment consists of images involving withdrawal, forsaking, hiddenness, or giving the people up. As the people remove themselves from God, God engages in major efforts at healing the breach, but may finally be forced into a tearful withdrawal, reluctantly allowing all the forces that make for death and destruction to have their way with the people. But, while God may give them up, God does not finally give up on them.[22]

God also suffers *with* his people, and some of the most poignant divine laments in the prophetic writings are over those who stand outside the covenant. Amidst the mourning of the people of Moab, God says, "My heart cries out over Moab" (Isa 15:5). Similarly, Jeremiah 48:31–32: "Therefore I wail over Moab, for all Moab I cry out, I mourn for the people of Kir Hareseth. I weep for you, as Jazer weeps." That God is depicted mourning over the fate of non-Israelite peoples as well as Israelites demonstrates that Israel has no monopoly on God's empathy. Even as the neighbouring nations are recipients of his judgments for their pride and cruelty, their peoples are also the objects of his compassion. And texts such as Isaiah 19:23–25, Jeremiah 12:14–15 and Jonah 4:10–11 speak of the universal compassion of Yahweh and hold out the promise of their blessing in ways similar to the eventual restoration of covenant Israel.

In this context, it is worth observing, too, that just as God takes delight in those who put their trust and hope in him (e.g. Pss 147:11; 149:4), there are numerous Old Testament texts that refer to him being "burdened" or "wearied" by the unrelenting disobedience of his people (e.g. Isa 1:14; 7:13; 43:24).[23] By his long-suffering restraint, holding back the day of his judgment, God in some sense bears their sin by internalizing their rejection of him. The intensification of suffering erupts not only in judgment but in the creation of new possibilities. This comes out strikingly in an oracle during the exile in Babylon, when, addressing the chaotic state of Judah, God says:

22. Fretheim, *Suffering of God*, 126.

23. Fretheim, 140–141.

> For a long time I have kept silent,
> I have been quiet and held myself back.
> But now, like a woman in childbirth,
> I cry out, I gasp and pant . . .
> I will lead the blind by ways they have not known,
> along unfamiliar paths I will guide them;
> I will turn the darkness into light before them
> and make the rough places smooth.
> (Isa 42:14, 16)

The labour pains bring forth a new world order (42:9). The prophet has just introduced us to the enigmatic Servant of Yahweh (42:1–7). Just as the justice-rendering work of the Servant reflects God's commitment to justice, so the vicarious suffering of the Servant in 53:4–10 reflects the suffering of God and is the means whereby God effects the salvation of the world.

So, instead of speaking (as does Kitamori) of an internal conflict of love and wrath in the being of God that results in the divine pain, it is better to say that there are intricate, multiple movements of pain which are described poetically as struggle. Love unrequited, goodwill frustrated, the reluctant "giving up" of people to the self-destructive consequences of sin, and the decision to restore and heal are all sources of pain in God.

Walter Brueggemann argues that grief, pain and lament are what generate hope rather than despair. Prophetic pathos cuts through institutional and social denial, and every attempt to cover up a real crisis in the divine–human relationship. Until pain is articulated, there can be no move to renewal: "Newness comes precisely from expressed pain. Suffering made audible and visible produces hope, articulated grief is the gate of newness, and the history of Jesus is the history of entering into the pain and giving it voice."[24]

Jesus and Divine Suffering

It is difficult, even well-nigh impossible, for those of us who are not first-time readers of the New Testament to experience the shockingly disorienting character of the Gospel narratives. We may, on every fresh reading, pick up significant details previously missed. But familiarity desensitizes us and dedramatizes the story since we know how it will end. Moreover, popular

24. Walter Brueggemann, *The Prophetic Imagination*, 2nd ed. (Minneapolis, MN: Fortress, 2001), 91.

evangelical preaching tends to reduce the entire narrative to the death on the cross which is presented in abstract formulas (e.g. "Christ died for our sins") disconnected from all the preceding drama; and the resurrection, while presenting "proof" of the truth of the gospel, is scarcely seen as central to its content. This double blindness – divorcing the death of Jesus from his life, and his resurrection from his death – has led to a tragic impoverishment of Christian witness.

The greatest contribution of late twentieth-century New Testament scholarship was to recover Jesus as a recognizably Jewish figure and to situate the Gospels within the world of Jewish apocalyptic hopes and Roman imperial power. Behind their divergences, the Synoptic Gospels share a common pattern. They tell the story about Jesus, not as an inexplicable divine irruption into history, but as the climax to the much longer story of Israel which is the focal point of the Creator's dealings with his world. This is the foundation story of the new Christian communities, scattered around the Mediterranean world, that are being addressed and who are called to take this story forward as they indwell its final act.

Many Jews, both in Palestine and in the diaspora, looked forward to a new and better age. Their hopes centred on the restoration of the people by their covenant God, the building and purification of the temple and Jerusalem, the defeat or conversion of the Gentiles and the establishment of purity and righteousness. "When that happened, Israel would no longer be dominated by the pagans. She would be free. The means of liberation were no doubt open to debate. The goal was not."[25]

Jesus of Nazareth takes those hopes in a new direction, while still being recognizably rooted in Israel's prophetic traditions. The reign of God which he claimed was being enacted in his person and ministry ruptures the status quo, just as new wine bursts old wineskins. Tom Wright invites us to focus on a

> young Jewish prophet telling a story about Yahweh's returning to Zion as judge and redeemer, and then embodying it by riding into the city in tears, symbolizing the Temple's destruction and celebrating the final exodus. I propose, as a matter of history, that Jesus of Nazareth was conscious of a vocation: a vocation, given him by the one he knew as "father," to enact in himself what, in Israel's scriptures, God had promised to accomplish all by himself. He would be the pillar of cloud and fire for the people of the new

25. N. T. Wright, *Jesus and the Victory of God* (London: SPCK, 1996), 151.

> exodus. He would embody in himself the returning and redeeming action of the covenant God.[26]

Jesus dismisses the pretensions of the Jewish religious establishment (e.g. Mark 11:27 – 12:12) and marginalizes Roman authority (12:13–17). He weeps over the beloved city, and pronounces not the purification of its temple (the central defining symbol of national identity) but its destruction and replacement by his own body. He weeps with other mourners at the grave of his friend Lazarus, but unlike them also gives vent to deep-seated outrage and indignation at death itself. The cries of the demon-possessed are signs of a cataclysmic upheaval of the social and cosmic order: "What do you want with us, Jesus of Nazareth? Have you come to destroy us?" (1:24). Jesus expels the demons with hardly a conflict, and the battle is over virtually before it can begin. God has mounted a decisive campaign against the powers of evil that torment humanity. But the campaign is waged in an utterly unexpected way, and culminates in the final confrontation on the cross.

Jesus's attitude to lepers is often missed in our reading of the healing miracles. But leprosy was not simply a cruel disease, it was an expression of social exclusion and isolation. And Jesus's embrace of lepers was typical of what God's liberating reign was all about: the empowering of the helpless, the restoration of the ostracized. Perry Burgess (1886–1962), an American Methodist preacher who devoted his life to the study and eradication of leprosy, wrote:

> From the beginning of recorded history its victims have suffered a fate more hideous than that of any criminal. Attacked by a disease that was rarely fatal but which often maimed and disfigured, its victims were objects of horror to themselves as well as to others. They were driven out of the land of the living, away from the company of their fellow men; forced to walk alone all the days of their lives; to bear in solitude their spiritual agony; to watch, uncomforted, their own physical disintegration. And the sentence was without hope, without end. No punishment so ruthless, so devastatingly final has ever been devised by the most vicious tyrant as the human race has inflicted upon these unhappy people.[27]

---

26. Wright, *Jesus and the Victory of God*, 653.

27. Perry Burgess, *Born of Those Years: An Autobiography*, quoted in Theodore Plantinga, *Learning to Live with Evil* (Grand Rapids, MI: Eerdmans, 1982), 87–88.

Naturally, Jesus's subversive proclamation and practice provoked anger among those comfortable with the status quo. How could this be God's anointed liberator of Israel when his controversial activities threatened to bring the military might of Rome down on Israel (John 11:47–50)? Palestine was a tinderbox. More pressing than the wrath of God was the wrath of Rome. Ellen Charry sums up the controversy Jesus provoked:

> His militancy and divisiveness demanded utter loyalty that intentionally disrupted family, social, and economic life across the land. He did not argue points of law politely with the elders in order to arrive at consensus or majority rule, as was their orderly process of the development of the tradition, unsettling the populace with his "field preaching," agitating large crowds and setting them against their leaders. Jesus was not a team player. He did not play by the rules. On the contrary, he was a rude loose cannon when relations with Rome required authorized leadership to maintain order, and mediate prudently between a restive populace and its edgy occupiers . . . Finally, Jesus had to be sacrificed, not to appease God on our behalf as later theology would argue, but to appease Rome on Israel's behalf.[28]

In his opening chapter, the evangelist Mark uses the word *euthys* ("immediately") no less than eleven times. We are plunged into a campaign, breathless in its pace, as the kingdom of God unfolds in the public ministry of Jesus. It's like "watching a multi-media presentation in which slides flash across the screen so rapidly that there is no time to absorb the details; we perceive the forward thrust of events and find ourselves caught up in them. Mark's Jesus has no time for leisurely discourses about the lilies of the field. This Gospel plunges us into the midst of a cosmic conflict careening forward; if we want to follow the story, we need to pick up the pace."[29]

Although the word "immediately" recedes after this opening chapter, Mark gives the reader the strong impression that events were moving forward with a momentum generated and sustained by Jesus. Through both word and action, Jesus is initiating events and transforming lives – calling fishermen and toll collectors to leave their jobs, healing the sick, restoring a demon-possessed

28. Ellen T. Charry, "The Uniqueness of Christ in Relation to Jewish People: The Eternal Crusade," in *Christ the One and Only*, ed. Sung Wook Chung (Milton Keynes: Paternoster; Grand Rapids, MI: Baker, 2005), 144.

29. Richard B. Hays, *The Moral Vision of the New Testament: A Contemporary Introduction to New Testament Ethics* (New York: HarperCollins, 1996), 89.

man, feeding two large and hungry crowds, stilling a storm, raising a dead girl to life, appointing and sending out twelve apostles, and so on. Mark's style of writing is to pack a whole lot of active verbs in describing Jesus. This extends to depicting Jesus's thoughts and feelings. For instance, he *knew* that the teachers of the law were upset at his claiming the authority to forgive, and also that power had gone out from him when a woman touched his garment; not only did he teach a large crowd, but he had *compassion* on them; and he was *indignant* when the disciples tried to prevent children from being brought to him. Jesus is the primary subject of the narrative. His deeds, thoughts and feelings are centre stage.

However, a remarkable change occurs in Mark's narrative from the moment Jesus is "handed over" to the priestly authorities in the garden of Gethsemane until his death on the cross. Now there is nothing that is explicitly attributed to his activity. His thoughts and feelings are no longer disclosed. Grammatically, he is the subject of only nine verbs, while he is the object of fifty-six. Furthermore, of the nine subject verbs, four are negative (three denoting his silence, and one his refusal to accept relief); four are verbs of speaking, but his words are misunderstood or disregarded – including the affirmation of his messiahship in response to the high priest's question (14:62) and the cry of dereliction on the cross, "My God, my God, why have you forsaken me?" (15:34); and the final verb is "he breathed his last."[30] The psalms of lament are alluded to often in the passion narrative, and Jesus in his anguish is identified with all who die questioning why God has left them to suffer alone.

Is Mark now telling a different story, or is Jesus no longer at the centre of the story? No. Rather, from the time of his being "handed over," Jesus's presence at the centre has taken a different form. He is now the *object* of other people's actions, not the active and initiating subject; not the agent, but the recipient; no longer working, but waiting in silence. He is not in control, but has now passed into the hands of others.

What is the relevance of this to us? Imagine a person who is struck down in the prime of life by a serious accident or debilitating illness. Up to that point in his life, he was in charge: arranging his own affairs, making decisions, planning projects and perhaps even the lives of others around him. Suddenly, his world has changed. He is no longer in charge of his own life; he has been

30. This shift in the narrative has been noted by Markan scholars, but a readable and detailed account is the centrepiece of W. H. Vanstone, *The Stature of Waiting* (1982; London: Darton, Longman & Todd, 2004), which I follow. However, while Vanstone criticizes the popular Christian emphasis on the death of Jesus at the expense of the passion, he is guilty of doing the exact opposite in rejecting any atoning significance in the cross.

"handed over" to other people and has become dependent on their decisions and actions. If he is hospitalized, he is confined to a bed with intravenous drips and all manner of tubes connecting his body to various machines. He may be anaesthetized and operated upon. If he has suffered a stroke, he is partially paralysed and may be unable to communicate; or, if he is in a terminal condition, he is injected with morphine and other drugs of whose effects on his body he is completely unaware. From being relatively self-sufficient and independent, he has become the object of the decisions, care and treatment of doctors, nurses, administrators and other family members.

While this transition from healthy person to immobilized patient is dramatic and not a universal experience, many of us – unless we are killed instantly or die peacefully in our beds – will make a similar transition, albeit less dramatically, through the gradual changes brought about by ageing or bereavement. We accept the inevitability that, towards the end of our lives, we will enter a "second childhood" in which we shall be as dependent on others as we were in our infancy. This passivity, no less than our agency while fit and active, is part and parcel of the human condition. But does this transition to a state of radical dependence, receptivity or passivity imply a diminution of our human worth and an affront to our dignity?

This is a central question in medical ethics today. Are Alzheimer patients no longer human persons? Does functional dependence legitimate euthanasia or assisted suicide? Some traditional Christian interpretations of the *imago Dei* (Gen 1:26–27), such as equating the image of God in humanity with rationality or the command to exercise dominion (often called "the cultural mandate"), have not been able to counter the widespread modern identification of human worth and respect with individual enterprise, achievement and autonomy. There is a clear contradiction here between the latter position and the language of human rights which is based on the intrinsic dignity of all human beings: "Intrinsic human dignity, if it indeed exists, cannot be a degreed property like rationality, intelligence, good looks, height or weight. For these are accidental properties that by their very nature change, develop, diminish or cease to be actual over time for the human being who has them. But that means that the human being is logically prior to its accidental properties, for the human being subsists as a unified being through all the changes it undergoes."[31] Moreover, in a more explicitly theological perspective, Rowan Williams notes that "Human dignity, the unconditional requirement that we attend with reverence to one

31. Francis J. Beckwith, "Dignity Never Been Photographed: Scientific Materialism, Enlightenment Liberalism, and Steven Pinker," *Ethics & Medicine* 26, no. 2 (Summer 2010): 97.

another, rests firmly on this conviction that the other is already related to something that isn't me. And without that conviction we are in serious ethical trouble."[32]

Mark began his narrative with the proclamation of Jesus Christ as "the Son of God" (1:1). Towards the end of that narrative, the Roman executioner of Jesus declares in wonder, without any prompting, the same confession. This, in Mark's hands, is prophetic irony. The Roman soldier is the only human character in this Gospel who uses the title Son of God. Obviously, the words carried a different meaning on his lips: he was recognizing Jesus, in Hellenistic fashion, as a divine hero, probably because of the courage and dignity he saw displayed (Luke expresses his words as "Surely this was a righteous man"). But his words carried a greater significance than he realized. While the Sanhedrin, representing the household of God, rejected their Messiah, here is a Gentile, and an agent of the oppressing foreign power, who responds positively. It prefigures the launching of the Gentile mission. Moreover, it is at the cross – and through the cross – that Jesus's identity is revealed and God's glory manifested.

In a slightly different but related context, Williams draws our attention back to the silence of Jesus before the Jewish high priest and the Roman governor Pilate. Jesus is precisely in the position of someone "who has been reduced to silence by the violence and injustice of the world he is in." But now,

> his silence, his complete presence and openness, his refusal to impose his will in a struggle, becomes a threat to those who have power – or think they have power. "For God's sake, talk to me!" says the High Priest, more or less . . . And Pilate's wonderment, bafflement and fear in the face of Jesus's silence are a reminder that, in this case, Jesus as it were takes the powerlessness that has been forced on him and turns it around so that his silence becomes a place in the world where the mystery of God is present.[33]

Williams concludes that in all our theological reflections on the person of Jesus, "it's essential that we should let them lead us back to that moment of Jesus before his judges, that moment when *nobody knew what to call him*, because there were no words for God made human. What faced Caiaphas and Pilate was something so much out of any imaginable intellectual world that there was nothing to be said."[34]

---

32. Rowan Williams, *Being Human: Bodies, Minds, Persons* (London: SPCK, 2018), 38.
33. Williams, *Being Human*, 95–96.
34. Williams, 97; emphasis original.

Yet, despite this caveat, tons of theological ink have been poured out in trying to articulate the mystery of a divine incarnation culminating in death by crucifixion. And articulate we must, though humbly admitting the limits of human thought and language, if the unbelieving world is to hear and welcome it as good news. In the cross, God crosses over the chasm that separates the Creator from creatures, the Holy One from sinners. It is both the "handing over" of God's own Son in vicarious judgment via the act of his being "handed over" to death by a God-defying humanity embodied in the highest representatives of religion and politics; and God's solidarity with all who suffer likewise as victims, both "sinners" and those "sinned against" by idolatrous religion and politics. He dies both *at our hands* and *with us*.

For this is the significance of crucifixion. While not perhaps the most painful way to die in the ancient Roman world, it was viewed as the most shameful. It was the form of capital punishment reserved for the "scum" of the empire, a way of not only destroying the body but obliterating every memory of the crucified one. The great senator and orator Cicero declared that "the very word 'cross' should be far removed not only from the presence of a Roman citizen but from his thoughts, his eyes and his ears."[35] That's why not a single ancient historian pays attention to crucifixion. It was the brutal underside of the Pax Romana, a way of forgetting the people who paid the price for the benefits Roman citizens enjoyed and the comfortable illusions about their civilization that they promoted.

However, for the post-Easter church, this is the turning point of history. This shameful death of an obscure outcast, unnoticed by any Roman historian, is the point at which God has broken the power of evil in his world and opened the way for freedom for all. Instead of being another of the countless forgotten victims, Jesus was remembered, and his story told and retold for centuries to come. His solidarity with all other forgotten victims, victims of terror and torture, all who are considered dispensable to protect the security and comforts of those who think they matter, enables them to be remembered too.

What does this imply for Christian conversion? Simply that there can be no conversion to Christ that does not entail, at the same time, a conversion towards the men, women and children at the bottom of our societies who bear the costs of the peace, wealth and security enjoyed by the few at the top. This will involve a reorientation of intellectual perspective, a cultivation of compassion, and a resolve to identify publicly with them in their situation

35. Cicero, *Pro Rabirio* 5.16, quoted in Martin Hengel, *The Crucifixion of the Son of God* (London: SCM, 1986), 134.

and to deploy tirelessly whatever gifts with which we have been endowed to address the causes of such social and economic exclusion.

What does this imply for our understanding of God? Martin Luther broke with tradition in boldly speaking of the *crucified God*. The words of the fourth-century Greek theologian Gregory of Nyssa were frequently cited in subsequent centuries: "The pure and undefiled takes on the stain of being human, and, passing through every stage of the deep poverty of human life, comes so far as to have experience of death. Look and see the measure of His voluntary poverty – that Life should taste death."[36] The Fathers truly struggled to hold to both the reality of the incarnation and the impassibility that they thought was indispensable for God to be God. But few within the "orthodox" Chalcedonian churches were able to make the breakthrough.

As the historian Peter Brown remarks:

> Some time in the 470s, Peter the Fuller, a hotly contested Monophysite patriarch of Antioch, deliberately added a phrase to the traditional litany of praise which addressed Christ as God. To the phrase, "Holy God, Holy and Mighty, Holy and Immortal One," he added, "Who was crucified for us." To upholders of Chalcedonian orthodoxy, this addition betrayed a blasphemous confusion of thought. No one could say that God Himself had died on the cross. Yet for the Antiochenes, there were times when God needed to be reminded, in no uncertain terms, that he had shared human suffering with those who now turned to him in prayer in times of catastrophe – of which the most dreaded, of course, were the earthquakes that occasionally shattered the towns of northern Syria . . . The addition "Who was crucified for us" guaranteed that the Monophysite God was intimately connected to the afflicted world.[37]

The Christian understanding of God as Trinity, and not an undifferentiated unity, sprang out of the experience of God's work of salvation in time and space and focused in Jesus of Nazareth. Speaking about a second "person" distinct from the Father, and a third who proceeds from both, stemmed from placing the cross, resurrection and ascension of Jesus at the centre of any discussion of the nature of God. However, the full implications of seeing suffering and death

---

36. Gregory of Nyssa, *On the Beatitudes*, in Peter Brown, *Poverty and Leadership in the Later Roman Empire: The Menahem Stern Jerusalem Lectures* (Hanover, NH: University Press of New England, 2002), 94.

37. Brown, *Poverty and Leadership*, 109.

as not isolated experiences of the Son in his human nature, but experiences in which the entire Godhead participates, has only come to be fully recognized in the twentieth century.[38]

To believe that the Creator God was uniquely present in the crucified Christ means to believe that God has chosen to identify himself as God in a human corpse. He has chosen to define his deity in weakness. God is revealed not as the one who inflicts suffering or avoids suffering, but who suffers. But if "only a suffering God can help" (Bonhoeffer's famous phrase, quoted at the beginning of this chapter), then that God, while choosing freely to suffer with us, must also not be overwhelmed and defeated by suffering.[39] The latter is embraced not as an end in itself but as the means to fulfil God's aims for his creation and his relationship with it. Hence the resurrection of Christ and the "new creation" that it inaugurates are indissolubly linked with the crucifixion. We shall see later that the resurrection vindicates the one who suffered and died as the faithful Son/Servant of Yahweh, and also affirms the way of the cross as the only way of confronting evil.

In the Trinitarian event of the cross, there is a "giving-up" and a "being-given-up," God present in God-forsakenness. The cross is the furthest point to which a God of love can go – that is, to the uttermost depth of alienation and estrangement – and it carries a universal redemptive significance that God's sharing of other deaths does not have. The challenge for any theology of God's suffering is clearly spelled out by Paul Fiddes: first, "to think of a God who can be the greatest sufferer of all and yet still be God"; and, then, "to speak consistently of *a God who suffers eminently and yet is still God, and a God who suffers universally and yet is still present uniquely and decisively in the sufferings of Christ*."[40] He continues:

---

38. G. W. F. Hegel (1770–1831) gave a philosophical interpretation of Luther's "crucified God," speaking of God as Absolute Spirit who comes to consciousness of himself through immersion in the world, taking the nothingness of death into his being and overcoming it in favour of life. Good Friday was universalized into a Speculative Good Friday. The twentieth-century German theologians who have sought to do "theology from the cross" build on Hegel's system, but not uncritically. See Jüngel, *God as the Mystery*, 63–73; Jürgen Moltmann, *The Crucified God* (London: SCM, 1974), 34–36.

39. Bonhoeffer was content to affirm the hidden presence of the suffering God in his world, and to commend the secular style of life we should live in the light of it. But he did not explore the manner of God's participation in suffering and death. It has been left to others, such as the American "death of god" theologians William Hamilton and Thomas Altizer, the German theologians Jürgen Moltmann and Eberhard Jüngel, and the British theologians Paul Fiddes and Alan Lewis to do this, at the risk of being overly speculative. I have found the work of the last two most illuminating and helpful, not least in their criticisms of the other four.

40. Fiddes, *Creative Suffering*, 2–3 (emphasis original).

> The transcendence of a suffering God can only be understood as a transcendent suffering, not a transcendence beyond suffering. Only the thought of God as Trinity can make sense of transcendent suffering, for only a God who happens as an event of relationships can be both other than and yet inclusive of the world. He can include all suffering in himself as he includes all human relationships, yet he is other than the world in his unique suffering, taking our suffering into himself out of the depths of the more profound and terrible suffering which remains his own.[41]

The Swiss Reformed theologian Karl Barth (1886–1968) expanded Luther's theology of the cross and formulated the dialectical statement that the divinity of God is displayed most clearly in the lowliness of the cross, while the glory of man is displayed in the resurrection.[42] This cleverly reversed the classical view that it is the human nature of Jesus which suffers in the cross and the divine nature which breaks through in triumph in the resurrection from the dead. Rather, affirms Barth, God is most divine in his humility.

If this claim is true, then the cross becomes that point in human history where divine humility confronts and overcomes human hubris. God, enfleshed among us in self-abasement and self-emptying love, in fellowship with the outcast and the powerless, provokes the most violent hatred on the part of the religious and the powerful. Thus the "foolishness" of the cross is where human self-knowledge breaks through simultaneously with the knowledge of God. It strips us to the raw bone, unmasking our idolatries, foolish vanities and the pretence that our refusal to trust in God is due to lack of evidence rather than malformed wills and disordered desires.

Living with Suffering

In the way that Jesus inaugurates the reign of God, the Old Testament picture of God is thus affirmed, deepened and transformed. In line with the prophets and sages of Israel, evil is not something to be understood but to be fought.[43] But

41. Fiddes, 143.

42. Karl Barth, *Church Dogmatics*, IV/1, trans. and ed. G. W. Bromiley and T. F. Torrance (Edinburgh: T&T Clark, 1936–77), 555–558.

43. "We do not understand the why of evil. But we can understand that we cannot understand . . . A rational solution to the problem of evil would necessarily imply that evil was an integral part of the harmony that came forth from God! . . . But evil is disruption, discontinuity, disorder, alienness, that which defies description in creational terms (except negatively!). Seeking its causal explanation, its ontological reason, its why, is tantamount to

God the Warrior becomes the Crucified God, the One who receives in himself the full force of human violence. This receipt of evil is also, paradoxically, the conquest of evil, the defeat of principalities and powers. God turns it back upon itself. He makes the supreme crime, the murder of the only righteous person, the very operation that abolishes sin. "God responds in the indirect way that is perfectly suited to the ambiguity of evil," writes Henri Blocher: "He entraps the deceiver in his own wiles. Evil, like a judoist, takes advantage of the power of the good, which it perverts; the Lord, like a supreme champion, replies by using the very grip of the opponent. So is fulfilled the surprising verse: 'With the pure you show yourself pure; and with the crooked you show yourself perverse' (Ps 18:26)."[44] The tragedy of so much of Christian history can be traced to the forgetfulness, on the part of church leaders and Christian politicians, that God the Warrior became the Crucified God.

The story of Jesus's passion now becomes a paradigm for a fully human existence. We may not journey to Jerusalem as he did, pronouncing God's judgment on the temple and its rulers and reconciling the world to God through being executed as a common criminal. But our journeys into the world can be like his, in courageous yet vulnerable confrontation with the powers of our age. Our sufferings cannot be redemptive like his sufferings; yet all our sufferings may be conformed to those sufferings, and so lose their power over us.

Suffering, whether mental or physical, is both a feeling and a sense of helplessness in the face of being impacted by events or forces outside one's control. We have remarked that when God chooses to make our suffering his own – supremely and decisively, but not exclusively, in the passion of Christ – he is constrained by that suffering, but it has no power to overwhelm him because he takes it into his own being and redirects it to serve his purpose. Likewise, in the case of suffering that has been deliberately inflicted on us, the moment we accept and "own" the suffering, the person or persons who inflicted it lose all power over us. When the sufferer has lost her fear of suffering, she finds the strength to resist and protest against the injustice, even if only mentally.

The power of the story of God's suffering is that while our suffering may appear utterly senseless, we can place our story of loss alongside God's story and see what meaning (if any) emerges. We may come to see how a terrible

---

seeking, by the very nature of that seeking, to reconcile it with the rest, in other words to justify it. To understand evil would be to understand that evil is not ultimately evil." Henri Blocher, *Evil and the Cross*, trans. David G. Preston (Downers Grove, IL: InterVarsity Press, 1994), 103.

44. Blocher, *Evil and the Cross*, 132.

situation can be redeemed, and wait on God to see how he can bring forth something good out of tragedy. This joint work with God cannot be undertaken by any third party, lest it becomes another theological justification of suffering or encourages a passive acceptance.

Humans, unlike other animals, are *persons*, transcending themselves and yet belonging to themselves. They transcend themselves because they are more than their past and their present, more than anyone else's judgment of them, more than the causes that have shaped them, more than the social and cultural contexts that they inhabit. In the midst of all the givens of life, persons can introduce something new, whether in meaning or in action. They can reframe what happens to them, as well as deciding what they do or will commit themselves to doing. And even the youngest or most severely disabled of persons can be agents in the sense of shaping the relationships in which they live and impacting the lives of their families and carers.

Margaret Spufford wrote an extraordinarily moving book, *Celebration*, about her battle with brittle bone disease, a disease that was also passed on to her daughter. She knew from her own creative life and research as an academic historian the way work is constantly going awry; the documents point in the other direction, the evidence does not fit the hypothesis, the sentence structure comes out wrong.

> I seem to be fighting with a living organism, and I must be obedient to its own growth, and adjust to the way this minute creation of mine grows, while still giving it discipline and form. I even know that my own utterly unwanted experience of physical pain, and the emotional pain of nursing our daughter, which were in themselves entirely evil, have enriched my own academic work in a way that was unplanned and unforeseen. Those things which were amiss seemed to have been somehow woven into the fabric, not entirely to its detriment.

She recognized how imperfect growths in the creation of God took on a strange beauty all their own. "The twisted tree is often the one to stand and marvel at: it has been given something out of its twistedness. There is a new kind of beauty which is intrinsically painful, yet free from the grotesque. As for the twisted child, I had learned how every 'normal' response, so hard fought for, was felt as miracle, culmination beyond reasonable hope."[45]

45. Margaret Spufford, *Celebration* (Glasgow: Collins, 1989), 77.

While she still regarded her constant pain and that of her daughter as "an unmitigated evil," she also found it to be one of "somehow *absorbing darkness*" into her own person, her own body: "If we are able to do this, to act, as it were, as blotting-paper for pain, without handing it on in the form of bitterness or resentment or of hurt to others – then somehow in some incomprehensible miracle of grace, some at least of the darkness may be turned to light." She concludes:

> I loathe and detest my bone disease. I am often miserable, often shamefully discontented, often isolated, often lonely. I feel pain, and the fear does not grow less. But oddly, after twenty years, I can no longer wish that things were quite otherwise, except for my husband's sake. Learning to live with the disorder as creatively as possible has in the end formed the person I am, as historian, or mother, or oblate. I think I can say, without any trace of masochism, that the disease has indeed been a creative medium. I have tried to use the pain of it to remind me to try to focus on what is really important. And what is really important is adoration.[46]

I return to the essay on pain by Talal Asad with which I began this chapter. Asad points to recent research that indicates that what a person experiences as painful, and how, are themselves modes of living a relationship. "The ability to live such relationships over time transforms pain from a passive experience into an active one, and thus defines one of the ways of living sanely in the world." The secular emphasis on the human body as the locus of moral sovereignty makes it difficult, Asad argues, "to grasp the idea of pain as an imagined relationship in which such 'internal' states as memory and hope mediate sociality."[47] Moreover, the ability to live sanely after a traumatic experience depends on the responses of others. He cites a therapist, Susan Brison, whose experience with victims of rape and torture makes her conclude that "In order to construct self-narratives, we need not only the words with which to tell our stories but also an audience able and willing to hear us and to understand our words as we intend them. This aspect of remaking a self in the aftermath of tragedy highlights the dependency of the self on others and helps to explain

46. Spufford, *Celebration*, 92, 93.
47. Asad, "Thinking about Agency and Pain," 84.

why it is so difficult for survivors to recover when others are unwilling to listen to what they endured."[48]

For life to have personal meaning, Rabbi Jonathan Sacks claims, "there must be people who matter to us, and for whom we matter, unconditionally and non-substitutably."[49] William James, the great American philosopher-psychologist at the turn of the twentieth century, noted that

> No more fiendish punishment could be devised, were such a thing physically possible, than that one should be turned loose in society and remain absolutely unnoticed by all the members thereof. If no one turned around when we entered, answered when we spoke, or minded what we did, but if every person we met "cut us dead," and acted as if we were non-existent things, a kind of rage and impotent despair would before long well up in us, from which the cruellest bodily torture would be a relief.[50]

Clearly this has profound implications for our life as a church. If the Christian liturgy re-enacts the life, death and resurrection of a crucified victim, then the stories of other victims must be given space to be heard and incorporated into that liturgy. Failing to do so isolates the Christian account of God from the everyday lives of people, both within and outside the church; and, in so doing, becomes an account of a different God.

But even if, in failing to act as the body of Christ, the church betrays the gospel and its calling, the sufferers who are abandoned can still find companionship in their "suffering in suffering" (a phrase of Jürgen Moltmann's[51]) with the abandoned and risen Christ. For the only ultimately satisfying mental response to the problem of unmerited or disproportionate suffering is to believe that our Creator, through a wonderful and incomprehensible act of self-limitation, is present in the darkness of affliction, shares our pain, bears our sorrows and sustains us through it all, creating good in spite of evil, so expressing the true nature of his divine power.

In this regard, Giles Fraser draws our attention to "a passage of extraordinary sadness" in the voluminous work of Friedrich Nietzsche, perhaps

---

48. Susan Brison, "Outliving Oneself: Trauma, Memory, and Personal Identity," in *Feminists Rethink the Self*, ed. D. Meyer (Boulder, CO: Westview, 1997), 21–22, quoted in Asad, 83.

49. Jonathan Sacks, *The Dignity of Difference* (London/New York: Continuum, 2002), 157.

50. William James, *The Principles of Psychology* (Boston, 1890), quoted in Alain de Botton, *Status Anxiety* (2004; Harmondsworth: Penguin, 2005), 15.

51. The harshest aspect of suffering is the feeling of abandonment, of being left to suffer by a loving God. Moltmann, *Crucified God*, 46.

the most influential atheist of modern times. Here Nietzsche expresses his sheer loneliness, his desperate need for the comfort of another:

> The last philosopher I call myself, for I am the last human being. No one converses with me beside myself and my voice reaches me as the voice of one dying. With the beloved voice, with thee the last remembered breath of human happiness, let me discourse, even if it is only for another hour. Because of thee I delude myself as to my solitude and lie my way back to multiplicity and love, for my heart shies away from believing that love is dead. I cannot bear the icy shivers of loneliest solitude. It compels me to speak as if I were Two.[52]

Nietzsche's answer to loneliness was to imagine himself as two persons who could then comfort each other. "Nietzsche became his own imaginary friend. It can be no surprise then that the sort of salvation he sought to design for himself was a form of self-salvation."[53]

How refreshing it is to turn from Nietzsche's pitiful self-absorption to the L'Arche community pioneered by the French Roman Catholic layman Jean Varnier, not far from where Nietzsche often loved to wander. This is a community, now found in several countries, where volunteer carers live together with persons with severe learning disabilities (those whom Nietzsche despised) and create a new family together. The British Methodist theologian Frances Young brings out the prophetic, counter-cultural character of this community of severely disabled human persons and the vision of humanness that it embodies:

> In a world where achievement is highly valued, where the success of science has encouraged the idea that all ills can be overcome, death endlessly postponed and suffering alleviated, where the cult of sport has exposed perfect bodies, where there's been a reaction against bodily inhibitions and sexual repression, L'Arche has perceived beauty in incurably damaged bodies, treasure in vulnerable and fragile persons. In the everydayness of attending to bodily functions, feeding and defecating, washing and dressing, the sanctity of bodies has been acknowledged, but in a context in which their transformation is not through miracles but through

---

52. Friedrich Nietzsche, *Philosophy in the Age of the Greeks*, cited in Giles Fraser, *Redeeming Nietzsche: On the Piety of Unbelief* (London/New York: Routledge, 2002), 159–160.

53. Fraser, *Redeeming Nietzsche*, 160.

the recognition of God's love and power in mutual need. It's not simply that the strong help the weak; rather, the weak reveal our common essential vulnerability as human creatures . . . In the ordinary, everyday business of living together, the divine image is discerned, secreted in the ordinariness of clay pots that are breakable, but in their brokenness expose the treasure within.[54]

54. Frances Young, "Wisdom in Weakness," *Theology* 114, no. 3 (May/June 2011): 187.

4

God and Natural Evil

> All things affirm Thee in living; the bird in the air, both the hawk and the finch; the beast on the earth, both the wolf and the lamb; the worm in the soil and the worm in the belly.[1]

In Graham Greene's novel *A Burnt-Out Case* (1960), Dr Colin works among severely handicapped people at a leper colony run by Catholic priests and nuns. At the end of the book, Colin and the Father Superior stand together watching the appalling afflictions and grotesque mutilations of the lepers. Dr Colin turns to the Father and suggests that his God must be pained as he looks at the suffering of the world. The Father's riposte is: "When you were a boy, they can't have taught you theology very well. God cannot feel disappointment or pain." Colin replies, "Perhaps that's why I don't care to believe in him."

We have seen that there are compelling biblical and theological reasons to reject the classical doctrine of divine perfection understood as immunity to suffering and change. Might there be, similarly, equally compelling reasons to question the popular, if not exactly classical, view that the natural world is cursed and fallen, a theatre of divinely inflicted cruelty and death? In the nineteenth century, the novelist and Anglican clergyman Charles Kingsley (1819–75) strongly castigated this view:

> We have only, if we need proof, to look at the hymns – many of them very pure, pious, and beautiful – which are used at this day in churches and chapels by persons of every shade of opinion. How often is the tone in which they speak of the natural world one of dissatisfaction, distrust, almost contempt. "Disease, decay, and death around I see," is their key-note, rather than "O all ye works

1. T. S. Eliot, *Murder in the Cathedral* (New York: Harcourt Brace Jovanovich, 1935), 86.

> of the Lord, bless Him, praise Him, and magnify Him together." There lingers about them a savour . . . that this earth is the devil's planet, fallen, accursed, goblin-haunted, needing to be exorcised at every turn before it is useful or even safe for man . . . It is time that we should make up our minds what tone Scripture does take toward Nature, natural science, natural theology . . . when, longing to reconcile my conscience and my reason on a question so awful to a young student of natural science, I went to my Bible, what did I find? No word of all this.[2]

In the same lecture, Charles Kingsley faced head-on the arguments advanced in favour of the view against which he was protesting:

> It is said to us – I know that it is said: You tell us of a God of love, a God of flowers and sunshine, of singing birds and little children. But there are more facts in nature than these. There is premature death, pestilence, famine. And if you answer: Man has control over these; they are caused by man's ignorance and sin, and by his breaking of natural laws – what will you make of those destructive powers over which he has no control; of the hurricane and the earthquake; of poisons, vegetable and mineral; of those parasitic Entozoa whose awful abundance, and awful destructiveness in man and beast, science is just revealing – a new page of danger and loathsomeness? How does that suit your conception of a God of love?

Traditionally the term "natural evil" has been applied by many theologians and philosophers (1) in biology, to the presence of suffering, death and extinction in the animal world; and (2) in geophysics, to earthquakes, tsunamis, volcanic eruptions, hurricanes and other severe climatic events that wreak destruction on humans and other animals on a large scale. In this chapter, I shall challenge this language as seriously misguided.

Animal Predation

"What a book a Devil's chaplain might write on the clumsy, wasteful, blundering, low and horridly cruel works of nature," observed Charles Darwin

2. Charles Kingsley, "The Natural Theology of the Future" (1871), The Literature Network.

in a letter to a friend.[3] And Darwin's best-known current interpreter Richard Dawkins writes in his book *River Out of Eden*: "During the minute it takes me to compose this sentence, thousands of animals are being eaten alive; others are running for their lives, whimpering with fear; others are being slowly devoured from within by rasping parasites; thousands of all kinds are dying of starvation, thirst and disease."[4]

The wanton suffering inflicted by humans on animals is a symptom of human moral perversity; and it has raised questions for centuries as to why a good and all-powerful God permits it. The infliction of suffering on animals by other animals has received much less attention, until in recent years when it has come to cast doubt for many people, Christians as well as others, on the goodness of the temporal order God has established in creation.

The natural world is filled with animals that are biologically "designed" in their internal organs, instincts and every aspect of physiology to exist by consuming other creatures. From parasitic wasps to lions and tigers, these are irreducibly predatory. With the exception of human beings, killer whales are earth's most capable predators. When they evolved ten million years ago, half of the earth's whales and seals became extinct. As a result of global warming, killer whales have appeared in Arctic waters. Horrified Inuit describe them as voracious and wasteful killers that have reduced populations of some Arctic mammals by a third.

And yet all these creatures play a vital role in the cycles of life and death, the great economy of nature in which all creatures must die and in dying make it possible for other creatures to be. What may appear as "wasted" lives, from an ecological perspective – which diverges from the biologist's in focusing not on the individual organism nor even on the species but on the whole living system to which they all belong – is simply an expression of the dependence of everything on everything else. Unlike humans, nature recycles all its waste. God's perspective likewise is to provide for the whole *oikonomos*, not to maximize individual survival.

It is surprising how many thoughtful Christians assume that animal pain and death are a consequence of the human "fall." One is tempted to say that this is because of a pre-modern understanding of geology and palaeontology. But not so. It was not until the modern era in Europe that this view came to

3. Letter to J. D. Hooker (1856), quoted in Darrel R. Falk, "Theological Challenges Faced by Darwin," in *Darwin, Creation and the Fall: Theological Challenges*, ed. R. J. Berry and T. A. Noble (Nottingham: Apollos, 2009), 75.

4. Richard Dawkins, *River Out of Eden: A Darwinian View* (New York: Basic, 1995), 132.

prevail in (predominantly) Protestant circles. The magisterial Reformers and John Wesley departed, albeit inconsistently in their various writings, from most of the church fathers and medieval theologians in bemoaning the "fallenness" rather than rejoicing in the goodness of God's non-human creation.

John Calvin (1509–64), for instance, normally a scrupulous biblical exegete, declared that "The inclemency of the air, frost, thunders, unseasonable rains, drought, hail, and whatever is disorderly in the world, are the fruits of sin. Nor is there any other primary cause of diseases."[5] He also regarded "the existence of fleas, caterpillars, and other noxious insects" as a sign of "some deformity of the world, which ought by no means to be regarded as in the order of nature, since it proceeds rather from the sin of man than from the hand of God."[6]

Contrast this with Athanasius, writing twelve hundred years before Calvin:

> If then they ask why he was not revealed through other, better parts of creation, or why he did not use a better instrument such as the sun or moon or stars or fire or air, but merely a man, let them know that the Lord came not to show himself, but to heal and teach those who were suffering . . . Nothing then in creation was in error in its ideas about God, save man only. So, neither the sun nor the moon nor the sky nor the stars nor the sea nor the air changed their course, but knowing their creator and king the Word, they remained as they had been made. But men only turned away from the good and thenceforth invented nothings instead of the truth and offered the honour due to God and the knowledge of him to demons and men in stone.[7]

Consider, too, Thomas Aquinas (1225–74), the great medieval theologian-philosopher: "For man's sin did not so change the nature of animals, that those whose nature it is now to eat other animals, like lions and hawks, would then have lived on a vegetable diet."[8] Similarly, Basil of Caesarea (330–79) finds in nature a "wise and marvellous order" and notes that God, omitting nothing

5. John Calvin, *Commentary on the Book of Genesis* (1554), on Gen 3:18, cited in John J. Bimson, "Reconsidering a 'Cosmic Fall,'" *Science and Christian Belief* 18, no. 1 (April 2006): 64.

6. Calvin, *Genesis*, Gen 2:2.

7. St Athanasius, *On the Incarnation* 42, ed. and trans. Robert W. Thomson (Oxford: Clarendon Press, 1971).

8. Thomas Aquinas, *Summa Theologiae*, Part 1: 96, Art. 1, cited in Richard L. Fern, *Nature, God and Humanity: Envisioning an Ethics of Nature* (Cambridge: Cambridge University Press, 2002), 223.

necessary, gave "to carnivorous animals . . . pointed teeth which their nature requires for their support."[9]

In contrast to this ancient catholic tradition, the Intelligent Design movement advocate William Dembski believes that for theological reasons we must attribute "natural evil" to the sin of Adam and Eve, but for scientific reasons think of it as effective retroactively. In his foreknowledge, Dembski suggests, God decreed animal predation millions of years ago before the creation of humanity in order to somehow contain and punish human sin, not unlike firefighters making "backfires" in anticipation of a coming blaze. "God brings about natural evil," declares Dembski, "to free us from the more insidious evil in our hearts."[10] He is vague as to how this actually happens, but clearly Adam and Eve are held morally responsible for natural evil even before humanity appeared on the scene. The great predators, with their sharp incisors, talons, claws and digestive tracts capable of processing only meat, owe their existence to human sin.

Ronald Osborn pungently rebukes Dembski:

> What kind of creature would punish Adam and Eve's rebellion – whether retroactively or proximately – by bending the rest of his creation from a state of perfect peace into so many malign forms, supernaturally summoning into existence the snake's venom and the jaguar's teeth and commanding innocent creatures to begin devouring one another for the moral instruction or chastisement of humans? What would we think of a parent who decided that the best way to educate their child in the combustibility of fire was to place the family cat on the stove? The child might learn something about fire, to be sure. But what would they learn about their parent?[11]

Although Genesis 9:2–5 does give human survival priority over animal survival, the Noah narrative makes it plain that animals are valued for their own sake by their Creator. Noah the conservationist exemplifies the role of "dominion" that all humanity has been called to – namely, the responsible care of other creatures on the planet. Human wickedness continues beyond the flood, but now it occasions God's patient endurance rather than immediate

9. Basil of Caesarea, "Hexaemoron," cited in Fern, *Nature, God and Humanity*, 223.

10. William Dembski, *The End of Christianity: Finding a Good God in an Evil World* (Nashville: B&H, 2009), 50.

11. Ronald E. Osborn, *Death before the Fall: Biblical Literalism and the Problem of Animal Suffering* (Downers Grove, IL: InterVarsity Press, 2014), 138.

judgment. He is concerned for and commits himself to the protection of the animal creation as well as humanity.

In his 1940 book *The Problem of Pain*, C. S. Lewis rightly cautioned that whatever we say on the subject of animal suffering will be highly speculative as we have no direct access to the inner life of animals. He warned against the "pathetic fallacy" of reading into animal behaviour our own human moral experience, as when we apply terms such as "cruel," "selfish" or "vicious" to creatures who are simply following their biological instincts. When an eagle swoops on a salmon to feed its young, does it make sense to describe this as "cruel" or "selfish" on the part of the eagle and to mourn the "suffering" of the salmon? Lewis also reminds us that sentience and consciousness exist at different ontological levels. A sentient creature might pass through a series of discrete connected states; but lacking consciousness, and therefore subjectivity, it cannot form an *experience* of pain by connecting these states.

Lewis also invoked an ancient orthodox Christian tradition in seeing the problem of evil as predating the emergence of humans. There was a cosmic fall, involving rebellious angels, and this has left its corrupting imprint on the earth of living creatures. "If this hypothesis is worth considering," writes Lewis, "it is also worth considering whether man, at his first coming into the world, had not already a redemptive function to perform . . . It may have been one of man's functions to restore peace to the animal world, and if he had not joined the enemy, he might have succeeded in doing so to an extent now hardly imaginable."[12]

Attractive as Lewis's proposal regarding humanity's redemptive function is, his cosmic conflict theodicy leaves unresolved how these malignant powers originated and why God should have allowed them to wreak such havoc over such long periods of evolutionary history. Lewis also seems to be giving satanic agency more than its due. For when we turn to the Hebrew Bible and New Testament there is no hint that animal pain and predation are "natural evils" and markers of a material creation corrupted by demonic powers.

The God who addresses Job from out of the "whirlwind" takes full responsibility for the wildness and ferocity of nature in all its multifarious and bewildering forms. He carves a "channel for the torrents of rain and a path for the thunderstorm" (Job 38:25), provides meat for young lions and the ravens (38:41), and commands the eagle to "build its nest on high" from where it "looks for food" so that "its young ones feast on blood, and where the slain are, there it is" (39:27, 29–30 NIV). And in the great paean of praise

12. C. S. Lewis, *The Problem of Pain* (1940; London: Collins, 1957), 124.

to the God of nature, Psalm 104, we read: "The lions roar for their prey, and seek their food from God" (104:21).

Whatever our philosophical views on the perception of pain, it is scientifically accepted that the sensation of pain has evolved as an indispensable survival mechanism in the higher animals, including humans. The mammals whose nervous systems were deficient and failed to pass urgent messages back to the brain are presumably among the species that became extinct and failed to pass their genes on to us. "Without pain we would be walking around on broken legs, happily going to school with meningitis, merrily ignoring fatal tumours and munching on broken glass with rotting teeth. In short, our lives would be considerably briefer than they are now."[13]

Moreover, pain can only exist where there is an integrated nervous system to mediate it and process signals from damaged tissue. This means that the vast majority of the world's living species are excluded from the possibility of suffering. And, even in the case of animal predation, predators have evolved to catch and kill prey as quickly and as efficiently as possible, either causing death at once or paralysing the nervous system with one blow so that death immediately follows.[14] And the overwhelming majority of prey are not killed by predators but die of sickness or old age. Colourful metaphors such as "the struggle for existence" and "Nature, red in tooth and claw," beloved of popular TV wildlife documentaries, are dangerously misleading. As for the "survival of the fittest," this was a term introduced by T. H. Huxley ("Darwin's Bulldog") as part of his anti-religious polemic and applied to human society. It was never used by Darwin himself in *The Origin of Species*. The "fittest" in any case has to do with reproductive success, and the proper technical terminology is "differential reproduction."

It is to the Victorian poet Alfred, Lord Tennyson that we owe the gloomy view of a "Nature, red in tooth and claw." However, another Alfred – Alfred Russel Wallace, the field naturalist and co-founder with Darwin of evolutionary theory – was of a very different opinion. In a section entitled "The Ethical Aspects of the Struggle for Existence" in his 1889 book *Darwinism*, Wallace dismissed as a "great exaggeration" Huxley's views of the "torments" and

---

13. Denis R. Alexander, *Rebuilding the Matrix: Science and Faith in the 21st Century* (Oxford: Lion, 2001), 353–354.

14. See the references in Jon Garvey, *God's Good Earth: The Case for an Unfallen Creation* (Eugene, OR: Cascade, 2019), ch. 11. Of course, even if animal suffering is significantly less severe and widespread than human empathy would lead us to believe, this does not warrant gratuitous human violence against any animal or the treatment of animals as mere commodities. We are part of an interconnected web of life that deserves respect.

"miseries" suffered by herbivorous creatures at the hand of carnivores. These were, said Wallace, "the reflection of the imagined sensations of cultivated men and women in similar circumstances; and . . . the amount of actual suffering caused by the struggle for existence among animals is altogether insignificant."

"We must remember," he continued, "that animals are entirely spared the pain we suffer in the anticipation of death – a pain far greater, in most cases, than the reality. This leads, probably, to an almost perpetual enjoyment of their lives; since their constant watchfulness against danger, and even their actual flight from an enemy, will be the enjoyable exercise of the powers and faculties they possess, unmixed with any serious dread." Wallace concluded that "the popular idea of the struggle for existence entailing misery and pain on the animal world is the very reverse of the truth"; and he quotes Darwin's own words from the third chapter of *The Origin of Species*: "When we reflect on this struggle, we may console ourselves with the full belief that the war of nature is not incessant, that no fear is felt, that death is generally prompt, and that the vigorous, the healthy, and the happy survive and multiply."[15]

Selection, Waste and Extinction

It is to Darwin that we owe the idea that the descent with modification of all living things was mainly driven by processes of natural selection, in which the overproduction of offspring leads to competition for limited resources, and out of the variety of individuals in a population some are found to be at a "selective advantage" over others. In fact, reproduction seems an utterly wasteful and inefficient process. For instance, out of ten thousand eggs laid in a frog's lifetime, on average only two survive to breed. Fourteen out of sixteen starlings die without breeding. Human biology is no less wasteful: in an ejaculation of up to two hundred million genetically unique sperm, only one will fertilize a genetically unique egg, if there is an egg around; and only just a third of fertilized eggs will produce a baby. The explanation of these numbers is to be found not only in predation (not at all in the human case), but also in the number of abnormalities that inevitably arise from genetic (including chromosomal) mutation, which is the fundamental process that drives all evolution and which, in so far as it is largely unrelated to the needs of the organism, may be properly described as "chance."

15. Alfred Russel Wallace, *Darwinism*, 2nd ed. (1889; London: Macmillan & Co., 1897), 37–40.

However, evolution – contrary to common belief – is not a "chance" process in the sense of being entirely indeterminate and unpredictable. Genetic mutations are not random in a mathematical sense because they are not evenly distributed across the genome. "The possibility that evolutionary processes might at some level be predictable would certainly have been deemed heretical had it been mentioned in a previous era, but now it's quite commonplace to find such claims in the literature. How times have changed."[16] Richard Dawkins, Darwin's most eloquent popularizer, has also emphasized this:

> Living things are too improbable and too beautifully "designed" to have come into existence by chance. How, then, did they come into existence? The answer, Darwin's answer, is by gradual, step-by-step transformations from simple beginnings, from primordial entities, sufficiently simple to have come into existence by chance. Each successful change in the gradual evolutionary process was simple enough, *relative to its predecessor*, to have arisen by chance. But the whole sequence of cumulative steps constitutes anything but a chance process.[17]

For the atheist Dawkins, however, this is an ultimately futile and "meaningless" process. But meaning is something that humans discover or impose on the world around them, and Christians and other theists choose to reframe evolution within a more expansive worldview.[18] No one who watches seagulls swooping and rising, or other examples of birds and animals at play (simply having fun!), is likely to believe that they are only taking the exact amount of exercise to improve their reproductive fitness. Moreover, Bishop John Taylor speaks for many in his wonder at so much of the natural world that we take for granted:

> The skill whereby a swallow navigates a six thousand mile flight from its winter quarters in a reed bed in South Africa to arrive at the same English cottage under the eaves of which it nested the previous year is but one of the breathtaking marvels of our "ordinary" world. So too are the powers of self-healing and recuperation latent in the human body upon which medical

16. Denis R. Alexander, *Is There Purpose in Biology? The Cost of Existence and the God of Love* (Oxford: Lion Hudson, 2018), 139. See further on that page for a summary of molecular constraints on genetic variation.

17. Richard Dawkins, *The Blind Watchmaker* (New York: W. W. Norton, 1986), 43.

18. For an excellent, popular introduction to evolutionary biology and how to situate it within a theological perspective, see Alexander, *Is There Purpose in Biology?*

> practice relies and which can also be activated by mental reorientation through prayer and other forms of "spiritual" therapy. "God," said Francis Bacon, "never wrought miracle to convince atheism, because his ordinary works convince it."[19]

Most of the species that have ever lived on this planet became extinct long before humans appeared on the scene. There may be as many as ten million species alive today, but these probably represent only a tiny proportion of those that have existed since life began. We do not know how most of these extinctions happened, but in many cases extremes of weather may have led to drought or ice-age conditions. Massive volcanic eruptions are likely to have obliterated certain local populations. It has been suggested that the disappearance of dinosaurs was caused by a large asteroid hitting the earth. As habitats change, organisms unable to adapt tend to die out. Stephen Jay Gould speculated that in the major catastrophe at the end of the Permian period, about 225 million years ago, up to 96 percent of all species existing at the time may have become extinct.

It is commonly said that it was wasteful for God to have created so many species that died out before the human age. But that is an anthropocentric view of creation, challenged (as we have seen) by many of the nature psalms and the closing chapters of Job. As Jon Garvey comments: "God can create things for their own sake, to last for a season – and the average life of a species, estimated as upwards of a million years, is 150 times longer than the age granted to the whole earth by young-earth creationists. And he can justly create them for a temporary role, such as the species believed to have 'terraformed' the earth's atmosphere with oxygen in the Precambrian era."[20] Further, the idea of "waste" is plausible only because of the biologist's artificial focus on the individual struggle to survive. But ecologically, nothing whatever is wasted, since everything depends on everything else (including plankton species recycling dolphin and shark waste). Garvey explains:

> Even the profligate "waste" of seed production is the reason for beautiful finches. God's perspective likewise is to provide for the whole *oikonomos*, not just to maximize individual survival. As for the prey species, we have no evidence that they prefer the biologist's perspective to God's or the ecologist's. It is only humans who leave behind mountains of waste to pollute the earth, and

19. John V. Taylor, *The Christlike God* (London: SCM, 1992), 221–222.
20. Garvey, *God's Good Earth*, 127.

> shoals of plastic bags to choke turtles. Nature has successfully recycled everything for four billion years.[21]

The biochemist Denis Alexander reminds us that carbon-based organisms (which are the only types that exist on Planet Earth) can only live by feeding on carbon-based molecules derived from other plants and animals. No multicellular animal can live by deriving all its energy needs from chemical elements – all are completely dependent on the food chain whereby organic molecules synthesized in other organisms are passed on to them.

> A world like our own without biological death of any kind would be a magical world, a nonsensical world by any understanding of the properties of matter. Even if an organism as relatively simple as a bacterium continued to divide in an unrestricted manner without death, its mass would soon fill the whole earth, its nutrients would become depleted and death would be inevitable. Carbon-based life and death are biologically so integrated that life is impossible without death.[22]

Perhaps we could add the observation that through pain and death other values have also been enhanced in the biosphere. We admire the lithe beauty of antelopes and springbok in their movements, forgetting that, in Holmes Rolston's resonant phrasing, it was "the cougar's fang" that "has carved the limbs of the fleet-footed deer, and vice versa."[23] Further, as Michael Pollan writes:

> Without predators to cull the herd deer overrun their habitat and starve – all suffer, and not only the deer but the plants they browse and every other species that depends on those plants. In a sense the "good life" for deer, and even their creaturely character, which has been forged in the crucible of predation, depends on the existence of the wolf . . . From the point of view of the individual prey animal predation is a horror, but from the point of view of the group – and of its gene pool – it is indispensable. So, whose point of view should we favour? That of the individual bison or Bison? The pig or Pig? Much depends on how you choose to answer that question.[24]

---

21. Garvey, 131.

22. Alexander, *Rebuilding the Matrix*, 353.

23. Holmes Rolston III, *Science and Religion: A Critical Survey* (1987; repr. Philadelphia/London: Templeton Foundation Press, 2006), 134.

24. Michael Pollan, *The Omnivore's Dilemma: A Natural History of Four Meals*, 322–323, quoted in Christopher Southgate, *The Groaning of Creation: God, Evolution, and the Problem of Evil* (Louisville, KY: Westminster John Knox Press, 2008), 6.

Furthermore, we can overstress the role of competition in natural selection. Random "genetic drift" (a mechanism that reduces genetic variation in a small population), sexual selection and geographical isolation are more benign factors in the evolutionary process. And *cooperation* (starting at the level of individual cells) is just as necessary for an organism's survival. Indeed, there is much more cooperation in biology than there is competition. An enormous step was taken in our evolutionary past when a eukaryotic cell, one with a true nucleus, came about through the cooperative union of two or three prokaryotes, cells without nuclei. Furthermore, biology is about organisms, not just molecules and cells; and organisms depend on ecosystems embedded in the biosphere, both of which are examples of large-scale cooperative behaviour between millions of species over long periods of time. Mutualism and symbiosis – organisms living together in a state of mutual dependence such as the bacteria in our guts, from which we benefit as well as they – are a universal feature of the biological realm. And the atmosphere on which we and all known animals depend was originally produced by single-celled bacteria patiently working for about two billion years to remove the methane that was the main constituent of the earth's early atmosphere and to turn enough of the carbon dioxide into oxygen.

Darwin himself was impressed by altruistic behaviour within and between species. The role of whole castes of sterile bees to help fertile bees to reproduce was a problem that troubled him for many years; and in the sixth edition of *Origin* he acknowledged that the wide extent of altruistic behaviour in insects and other creatures might prove fatal to his entire theory of natural selection.

Martin Nowak, Professor of Biology and Mathematics at Harvard University, has pointed out that new levels of organization evolve when the competing units on the lower level begin to cooperate. Genomes, cells, multicellular organisms, social insects and human society are all based on cooperation. He goes on to argue that "Cooperation is the secret behind the open-endedness of the evolutionary process. Perhaps the most remarkable aspect of evolution is its ability to generate cooperation in a competitive world. Thus, we might add 'natural cooperation' as a third fundamental principle of evolution besides mutation and natural selection."[25]

We are learning that evolution is a far more complex process than is presented in undergraduate biology textbooks, let alone popular science programmes. Although classic Darwinism is framed by referring to organisms

25. Martin A. Nowak, "Five Rules for the Evolution of Cooperation," in *Evolution, Games and God: The Principle of Cooperation*, ed. Martin A. Nowak and Sarah Coakley (Cambridge, MA: Harvard University Press, 2013), 99–114, at 110.

adapting to environments, the actual process of evolution involves the creation of new "ecological niches" as new life forms come into existence. Richard Lewontin observes that part of the ecological niche of an earthworm is the tunnel excavated by the worm and part of the ecological niche of a tree is the assemblage of fungi associated with the tree's root system that provides it with nutrients. He writes: "Despite the evidence that organisms do not simply use resources present in the environment but, through their life activities, produce such resources and manufacture their environments, the distinction between organism and their environments remains deeply embedded in our consciousness. Partly this is due to the inertia of educational institutions and materials."[26]

It is unsurprising that many of the features we associate with the human condition, notably tool making, cultures and emotions, are recognizable in a rudimentary form amongst some non-human animals. It is very likely that elephants, some of the higher apes, dolphins and domesticated dogs have an emotional life. We know that clans of female elephants, led by matriarchs, periodically associate in larger groups. So strong does elephant empathy seem that they sometimes bury their dead, and will return repeatedly to the skeleton of a deceased matriarch to caress her tusks and bones. Elephants have been known to extract spears from wounded friends, and to stay with infants born with disabilities.

Tim Flannery writes of a remarkable incident involving dolphins:

> The free-living dolphins of the Bahamas had come to know researcher Denise Herzing and her team very well. For decades, at the start of each four-month-long field season, the dolphins would give the returning humans a joyous reception: "a reunion of friends," as Herzing described it. But one year the creatures behaved differently. They would not approach the research vessel, refusing even invitations to bow-ride. When the boat's captain slipped into the water to size up the situation, the dolphins remained aloof. Meanwhile on board it was discovered that an expeditioner had died while napping in his bunk. As the vessel headed to port, Herzing said, "the dolphins came to the side of our boat, not riding the bow as usual but instead flanking us fifty feet away in an aquatic escort" that paralleled the boat in an organized manner.[27]

---

26. Richard Lewontin, "It's Even Less in Your Genes," *New York Review of Books*, 26 May 2011, 23. For the current debates within evolutionary theory (what mechanisms drive evolution), see Michael Burdett, "The Changing Face of Evolutionary Theory?," BioLogos, 2 March 2015.

27. Tim Flannery, "The Amazing Inner Lives of Animals," *New York Review of Books*, 8 October 2015, 20.

The anecdote raises fascinating questions: Can dolphin sonar penetrate the steel hull of a boat – and pinpoint a stilled heart? Can dolphins empathize with human bereavement? Is dolphin society organized enough to permit the formation of a funeral cavalcade?

Notwithstanding these observations, we need to state in the face of some versions of eco-theology that seek to reduce human beings to simply one species amongst others in the name of a supposed "biotic egalitarianism," that human beings, though biologically so clearly connected to the many millions of other species that make up the great tree of life, really are *profoundly different* – and not just from the world of chimpanzees but also from their closest extinct (hominid) relatives. Humans don't just make tools, they make tools that make other tools. They don't only utter auditory signs to communicate, they use language to create other worlds. And we are the only species that, invoking moral sensibilities, agonizes over the fate of other species. Whether other animals also have some sense of the sacred, the *numinous*, and whether this is mediated through human contact or independent of humans, is unanswerable. But if they do, we can be assured that the Creator's relationship with them is appropriate to their level of responsiveness.

Evolution and Eschatology

From a Christian perspective that sees the world as God's creation, evolution has been a means of producing an amazing diversity of life forms, both diachronically across aeons of adaptation and extinctions, and synchronically in the living web of interconnected ecosystems. Both the life-generating ecosystems that gave humans birth and also the other sentient creatures that share Planet Earth with us constitute an interlocking web of life.

Moreover, we can only understand the present creation from an eschatological perspective. The enigmatic statement in Mark 1:13 about Jesus being "with the wild animals" may be seen as an anticipation of a future world when "the dread of humanity" which has befallen the non-human world since the advent of humanity (see Gen 9:2) is removed. It comes on the heels of Jesus's identification as the messianic Son of God (Mark 1:11; cf. Ps 2:7) and his victory over the Satan; and it needs to be read against the background of Old Testament eschatological hopes, as expressed in Isaiah 11:6–9 (following the description of the coming Davidic Messiah in vv. 1–5), Job 5:22–23 and Hosea 2:18. In Jesus the messianic reign has dawned, and this reign includes the healing of enmity between humankind and the wild animals. Human dominion,[28] which was perverted into domination and exploitation by human sin, will be restored; and in Jesus's peaceful companionship with the wild animals we are given a foretaste of that eschatological restoration. Jesus neither terrorizes nor domesticates the wild animals. He is simply with them. And in that pregnant phrase "with the wild animals" Mark gives us a powerful reminder of the value of the non-human creation in the eyes of God. Human dominion, restored in Jesus (the new Adam), enables the wild animals to find their appropriate place in the wilderness as creatures who share God's world with us.

The well-known passage in Romans 8 also points in the same direction. A minority of commentators translate *ktisis* in verse 20 as "creature" rather than "creation," referring metaphorically to the human body that experiences futility and frustration as it awaits its glorious resurrection.[29] But the vast majority understand this text as pointing to the "reconciliation of all things" in Christ that the great Christological texts such as Colossians 1:15–20 and Ephesians 1 describe. It is "in hope" that the Creator has subjected the present world to decay and death. The present created order is *good but incomplete*; it was never the Creator's final word on his creation.[30] The latter is currently groaning as in the pains of childbirth, awaiting the dawn of a new creation in which it will find its created destiny, alongside the liberation and transformation of the human children of God. As to what aspects of the present creation this refers to, animate and inanimate, it is best to adopt a stance of *humble agnosticism.* All we can say is that like our own bodily resurrection there will be both continuity and discontinuity between the present world order and the new regenerate world order. The world will not be destroyed but transformed and suffused with the glory of the Triune God.

But in our environmentally sensitive age, theologians anxious to rid theology of its anthropocentric baggage have not been averse to throwing

---

28. In the Old Testament, kings are described as shepherds, those called to protect and nurture the people; and a righteous king was a good shepherd. The Hebrew verb translated "rule" or "have dominion" in Gen 1:28 has this implication.

29. See, for instance, J. Ramsay Michaels, "Redemption of the Body: The Riddle of Romans 8:19–22," in *Romans and the People of God*, ed. Sven K. Soderlund and N. T. Wright (Grand Rapids, MI: Eerdmans, 2000).

30. In popular Christian usage, the terms "good" and "very good" have been transmuted into "perfect." But, in context, they are best understood in a *functional* sense: good for the purpose of fruitfulness and growth. In any case, a "perfect" infant is one that we expect to grow into maturity, not remain in a static state.

caution to the winds and indulging in speculative theorizing. For Christopher Southgate, "[E]xtinction of a species means the loss of a whole way of being alive on the planet, a whole aspect of the goodness of creation, a whole way of praising God."[31] Compensation for the pains of existence, as well as fulfilment of their created potential cut short by premature death, are said to require that animals, too, share in the eschatological resurrection. Richard Fern argues that "while it may appear absurd to some to imagine dogs, cats, oaks and sycamores, spawning salmon and fungi, in heaven, theistic naturalism cannot imagine otherwise. Would we not lose our souls, our identity and purpose, in a world made barren by their absence? What might God provide that would compensate us for such a loss?"[32]

The physicist-theologian Richard Russell goes even further: "The challenge of evolution leads to the following criteria which eschatology must meet. First, it must include not only humanity and all the history of life on earth, but more than that: not only every species but even and most importantly the individual creatures of every species. For creatures suffer, not species, and thus creatures individually – one by one – must be the focus of any genuine Christian eschatology . . . and not as somehow included merely through human redemption."[33] Likewise, Denis Edwards: "God is with every sparrow, every beetle, every Great White shark, every creature hunting another for food and every creature that is the prey of another . . . Animals will reach their redemptive fulfilment in being taken up into the eternal life of the Trinity."[34]

Underlying this breathtaking boldness are unwarranted assumptions about the "suffering" of non-human creatures and what constitutes creaturely "fulfilment." It seems that whatever is transient carries no value – that value pertains only to that which is permanently enduring. I find this a strange argument. The notion that whatever comes into existence and passes out of existence has no value in itself is a notion more in tune with Hellenistic or Hindu-Buddhist philosophy than Judaeo-Christian. A musical note or chord is transitory, but it is what contributes to the making of the whole symphony.

---

31. Southgate, *Groaning of Creation*, 125.

32. Fern, *Nature, God and Humanity*, 205. He, like Southgate, clarifies that this applies only to sentient animals. "It does not follow that this holds true for living creatures in general nor that any non-humans will live forever in the sense true of human beings" (205–206).

33. Richard J. Russell, *Cosmology from Alpha to Omega* (Minneapolis, MN: Fortress, 2008), 266.

34. Denis Edwards, "The Redemption of Animals in an Incarnational Theology," in *Creaturely Theology: On God, Humans, and Other Animals*, ed. Celia Deane-Drummond and David Clough (London: SCM, 2009), 95.

And even if the symphony itself fades into oblivion (as do all cultural and technological artefacts), who would deny that it was deeply valued by many?

Moreover, an oak produces millions of acorns, with only one surviving to replace itself. Is each acorn to become a mighty oak in the new creation? A bullfrog can lay twenty-five thousand eggs in a clutch, and lay more than one clutch a season. Does the risen Jesus resurrect all these frogs? Even vegetarian lions and resurrected prey would have to eat shrubs and grass. When these resurrected vegetarians eat fruit, they kill the seeds within. If human life terminates at death, does that mean that a human life has no value at all? The saints of the Old Testament did not think so. I believe that every human being's life does not end with death, but I cannot make sense of extending this thought to every dinosaur or mastodon, let alone every rodent and cockroach I have killed.

In similar vein, Jürgen Moltmann declares that the raised body of Christ has a "transfiguring efficacy" that reaches to "animals, plants, stones, and all cosmic life-systems."[35] And elsewhere he writes: "There is no redemption for human beings . . . without the redemption of nature."[36] No matter that Romans 8 seems to put things the other way around: no redemption for nature without the redemption of human beings!

Moltmann further states:

> Not even the best of all possible stages of evolution justifies acquiescence in evolution's victims, as the unavoidable fertilizers of the future . . . There is therefore no meaningful hope for the future of creation unless "the tears are wiped from every eye." But they can only be wiped when the dead are raised, and when the victims of evolution experience justice through the resurrection of nature. Evolution in its ambiguity has no such redemptive efficacy and therefore no salvific significance either. If Christ is to be thought of in conjunction with evolution, he must become evolution's redeemer.[37]

I frankly don't know what biological, let alone philosophical or theological, sense can be made of notions like "victims of evolution" and Christ as "evolution's redeemer," given what was stated earlier about how evolution actually works.

---

35. Jürgen Moltmann, *The Way of Jesus Christ: Christology in Messianic Dimension* (San Francisco: Harper, 1990), 258.

36. Jürgen Moltmann, *The Coming of God: Christian Eschatology* (Minneapolis, MN: Fortress, 1996), 260.

37. Moltmann, *Way of Jesus Christ*, 296–297.

Richard Fern qualifies his statement about animal restoration by recognizing that what makes for a difference in the case of humans is "the fact that our physical processes issue in self-awareness and, thus, have no natural end: our capacity to learn and grow is unlimited; hence the case for an unending future. It may be, then, that insofar as non-human selves and sentients appear in the life-to-come, it will only be, as individuals, for a limited period of time, until they, too, are able to live a good life after their kind."[38] However, Moltmann, as Richard Bauckham observes, clearly regards all death in nature as unnatural, a tragic destiny. "At this point one may want to ask questions. Does death really have the same significance for every kind of creature? For elephants, who mourn their dead, it is a tragic destiny, as it is for us. But for this year's marigolds, which die in the annual cycle of death and new life that will produce next year's marigolds, is death tragic? Need we mourn the individual marigold as we certainly would the species, should it become extinct?"[39]

Lying beneath these vague invocations of "redeeming evolution" there seems to lie the ancient (but now discredited) conception of the human being as a "microcosm" of the larger cosmos.[40] This was brought into the Christian tradition by thinkers such as Gregory the Great, St Maximus the Confessor and Bonaventura. Certainly, the human body of Jesus, just like all our human bodies as well as those of animals, are animated stardust – all the elements that constitute our bodies were cooked in the sun's nuclear furnace. But what effect does the resurrected body of Jesus have on the processes of nucleosynthesis and the life and death of stars? We all carry the signature of our evolutionary ancestry in our bodies. But there are many evolutionary pathways, both fertile and dead-ends, that do not converge on the human body. How, for instance, does the resurrected body of Jesus participate in the life of plants? None of the distinctive characteristics of plants – rootedness in the soil, photosynthesis – is found in the humanity of Jesus.

The Danish theologian Niels Henrik Gregersen has coined the term "deep incarnation" to speak of Christ's transformative presence in the cosmos. He begins by stretching the meaning of *sarx* in John 1:14 to refer not only to human or even animal flesh, but to "the *whole malleable matrix of materiality.*"[41]

38. Fern, *Nature, God and Humanity*, 207.

39. Richard Bauckham, *The Theology of Jürgen Moltmann* (Edinburgh: T&T Clark, 1995), 210–211.

40. Indeed Moltmann states explicitly that humanity is "a microcosm in which all previous creatures are to be found again." *God in Creation* (Minneapolis, MN: Fortress, 1993), 186.

41. Niels Henrik Gregersen, "Deep Incarnation: Why Evolutionary Continuity Matters in Christology," *Toronto Journal of Theology* 26, no. 2 (2010): 176–177 (emphasis original).

The divine Logos has summed up not merely humanity, but "the whole realm of the material world from quarks to atoms to molecules, in their combinations and transformations throughout chemical and biological evolution." The implication is that "*God becomes Jesus, and in him God becomes human and (by implication) foxes and sparrows, grass and soil.*"[42]

For Gregersen, "it is as natural for God to dwell in the world of dirt and waste as it is for God to be present in the uniquely human characteristics of highly developed consciousness, morality, religious imagination, and God-consciousness."[43] However, this claim is so theologically vague that it borders on an irresponsible flirtation with pantheism. Surely terms like "natural" and "dwell in" demand more nuanced explication. What mode God's immanent presence in and for his creatures takes surely depends on the nature of the particular creature involved. His active presence in evil situations cannot be the same as his presence in the pursuit of truth and goodness, let alone his indwelling presence in the church. Given the diversity and subtlety of God's relationships with his creatures, trying to encapsulate these relationships within a single concept like "incarnation" is fraught with danger.

In a later essay Gregersen attempts to clarify what he means: "[T]he point of deep incarnation is not that God is, plainly speaking, 'incarnate in all that is,' but rather that the incarnate Logos, sent from God the Father, is present *with* and *for* all creatures, including in their sufferings. As such, the Incarnate One is indeed 'in all that is.'"[44] Gregersen's emphasis on prepositions is actually significant. For, in an essay in the same volume, Richard Bauckham points out that what distinguishes the uniqueness of the incarnation is that in the humanity of Jesus Christ, God was not simply *in*, *with* and *for* his creation, but came to us *as* the person Jesus Christ. "By incarnation *as* a particular human person, God is able to be *with* all other creatures, human and non-human, in their ecological interrelatedness in a way that affirms their immense diversity and makes God himself, incarnate as Jesus Christ, their unifying centre."[45]

It seems to me that Bauckham's "ecological interrelatedness" is a far better way of articulating how Christ's incarnation and resurrection benefits the non-human world than invoking our evolutionary history or trying to extend

42. Gregersen, "Deep Incarnation," 182 (emphasis original).

43. Gregersen, 185.

44. Niels Henrik Gregersen, "The Extended Body of Christ: Three Dimensions of Deep Incarnation," in *Incarnation: On the Scope and Depth of Christology*, ed. Niels Henrik Gregersen (Minneapolis, MN: Fortress, 2015).

45. Richard Bauckham, "The Incarnation and the Cosmic Christ," in Gregersen, *Incarnation*, 53.

arbitrarily the meanings of both incarnation and *sarx*. In order to be related to all other species, it is not necessary that humans should somehow sum up all other created natures in their own nature. This leaves room for recognizing diversity even in the destinies of present creaturely entities. Worms and viruses need not be resurrected. But perhaps elephants, dogs and dolphins will – but with what new biological natures, and obeying what physical laws, remains beyond our imaginative capacities!

Natural Disasters

An earthquake, followed by raging fires and tidal waves, struck the city of Lisbon on 1 November 1755. The sudden receding of the sea attracted crowds of onlookers to the shore, and they perished when the waves returned. The event shocked and fascinated the entire continent of Europe, and occasioned a widespread debate about the providence of God. John Wesley was among those who believed that such earthquakes had no natural explanation, but were acts of divine judgment on human sin. The deist Voltaire wrote a poem ridiculing the optimistic views of Leibniz,[46] and asking whether the vices of Lisbon were so much greater than those of London or Paris to merit such indiscriminate judgment from God. Unfortunately for Wesley's view, it appears that most of the brothels in the city and their occupants were unscathed while all the churches, in which thousands were celebrating All Saints' Day, were destroyed.[47]

Christians are not the only ones prone to making such statements. Rabindranath Tagore thought Mahatma Gandhi profoundly mistaken in his readiness to explain to his countrymen that the 1934 earthquake in Bihar (Eastern India) was a "divine chastisement" for persisting with the sin of "untouchability." Tagore wrote: "[W]e can never imagine any civilized ruler of men making indiscriminate examples of casual victims, including children and members of the untouchable community, in order to impress others dwelling at a safe distance who possibly deserve severer condemnation."[48] As Tagore

46. That is, that we live "in the best of all possible worlds."

47. See the description and discussion by David Fergusson, *The Providence of God: A Polyphonic Approach* (Cambridge: Cambridge University Press, 2018), 124–132. Fergusson points out that, contrary to Aquinas and many Jesuit theologians, Wesley held a "god-of the gaps" view of earthquakes (127).

48. Sabyasachi Bhattacharya, ed., *The Mahatma and the Poet: Letters and Debates between Gandhi and Tagore, 1915–1941* (Delhi: National Book Trust, 1997), 158, cited in Sunil Khilnani, "Nehru's Faith," 34th Jawaharlal Nehru Memorial Lecture, Delhi, 13 November 2002.

saw it, Gandhi's view sanctioned a kind of terrorism on the part of religion. When it came to explaining the natural world, Tagore was firm that reason and science had priority.

Whatever their historic origins, the various flood stories that are prevalent in many of the world's cultures reflect early humanity's sense of the precariousness of life. Human survival was threatened not only by germs and disease, but also by vast forces of nature capable of catastrophic destruction. Creation was constantly on the edge of chaos. For the Old Testament writers, it was only God's holding back of the "waters of chaos" (Gen 1:6–7) that guaranteed a space for life to flourish. The flood narrative of Genesis begins with God lamenting the depths of *human violence* on the earth, rather than animal ferocity or predation. God's decision to "undo" his creation, so to speak, is a painful one, made in grief more than in anger. It is the violence of humanity that has "corrupted the earth" (6:11, 13), a theme that has been highlighted from chapter 4 onwards with its account of the ambivalence of civilizational development.

When things go well, we simply don't believe in disasters. This is why rational self-interest and long-term prudence in the face of threats such as climate change and global warming are too feeble motives for most of us to change our ways of life for the sake of posterity. We need to suffer ourselves. Isn't it interesting how God does not enter the picture at all when the media reports, say, the growth of scientific understanding (including of earthquakes and tsunamis) or recent medical discoveries (these are attributed solely to human genius), but he so quickly becomes the scapegoat when things start going wrong, especially in the natural world?

One important question that is rarely raised is the following: why is it that when hurricanes and earthquakes hit places like Florida or Japan, the loss of life is minimal; but when the same disasters occur in the Caribbean or South Asia, the devastation is mind-boggling? The answer is simple and straightforward: *economic poverty*. Or economic poverty combined with corruption and incompetence on the part of government officials. In South Asia, annual warnings about floods and cyclones are routinely ignored when the technology needed to save lives and property is readily available. Coral reefs and mangrove swamps (that absorb much of the impact of tropical storms and ocean surges) have virtually disappeared from our coastal belts. Information collected by satellites and seismic warning systems owned by rich nations is not passed on to poorer nations. Poverty and economic inequalities on the scale seen in our world cannot be blamed on God. They represent a violation of God's will for humanity.

The Roman Catholic theologian Jon Sobrino, in a moving reflection on the two earthquakes that struck his country of El Salvador within a month of each other in 2001, observed that such tragedies serve as an X-ray of a country: "The earthquake has pointed out where sin, poverty, and injustice are most cruelly focused: on women and children, on peasant men and women, on those who have lost jobs and those who cannot get credit, on those who have practically no decision-making power over their own lives and future."[49] He pointed out that "An earthquake, like a cemetery, reveals the iniquitous inequality of a society, and thus also its deepest truth. Some tombs are huge, sumptuous pantheons of luxurious marble, in prestigious locations. Others, almost without names and without crosses, are piled up in hidden places and consigned to anonymity. They are the majority."[50]

Creation is the free decision of the Triune God, a gratuitous gift. Every act of creation, in human contexts of parenting, music or literature, involves both the exercise of power and the self-limitation of that power. We have seen in the previous chapter how creators respect the integrity of their creations, and that the relationship between creator and creation cannot be described adequately in the language of "controlling" and "ruling"; there is also a "letting-be," a willingness to let the creation unfold in its own way and according to its intrinsic character. Given the mystery in every creative act that great artists and musicians always confess, how much greater is the mystery when the topic is God's continuous creation of the world.

Modern science has given us a picture of God's world and of human life as evolving through a long process of potentialities being actualized in time. The world is not a closed, predictable system but a place where genuine *novelty* emerges, often in unpredictable ways. If the universe were a linear Newtonian mechanical system, the future would, in a very real sense, be contained in the present, and nothing genuinely new could happen. But in reality, our universe is not a linear Newtonian mechanical system. To recall an image that John Polkinghorne has used, our world is made up of clouds as well as clocks, and clouds are far more difficult to study than clocks. They are examples of what physicists call "chaotic" or non-linear dynamic systems, and most systems in the physical and biological world are of this type. Such systems still obey the universal laws of physics but their behaviour is intrinsically unpredictable as the possible solutions to the equations that describe them are indefinite.

49. Jon Sobrino, *Where Is God? Earthquake, Terrorism, Barbarity, and Hope*, trans. Margaret Wilde (Maryknoll, NY: Orbis, 2004), 69.

50. Sobrino, *Where Is God?*, 3.

They are enveloped in probabilities, but future options are constrained within specific limits (called "strange attractors"). The paths followed by such systems are irreversible, so that time now becomes significant, unlike in the mechanistic picture.[51]

Thus, physical reality is more subtle than was thought in earlier times. It is a complex interweaving of both contingency and necessity. Now if God has chosen to create us humans as part of such a world, then we have emerged, along with every other form of life on Planet Earth, out of the complex interactions of spontaneity and regularity. As physical beings, we share in the unpredictability and vulnerability of the rest of the created order. Human finitude and limitation are not evil; it is rather the rejection of limitation that constitutes sin. Our solidarity as a human species is what leads to our rejoicing in the joy of others and weeping over the pain of others. To only receive through the good that others do, but not to suffer the consequences of what others do, would be a denial of our interdependent creatureliness.

Suffering remains an unfathomable mystery, but we do not have to choose between a God who is an absentee landlord or one who is a puppet master. In relation to moral evil, Christian theology has long argued in terms of human free will: that despite the many disastrous choices humans have made, a world of freely choosing beings is better than a world of perfectly programmed automata. In relation to the physical world, God has brought about an ordered universe and allows it to "become itself," without constant intervention, while sustaining the entire process by his love and wisdom. Each created entity is allowed to behave in accordance with its nature, including the complex combination of order and spontaneity which is usually part of that nature. God wills neither the growth of cancerous tumours nor acts of terrorism, but he allows these to happen. The same process of gene mutations that leads to novel life forms also leads to the development of malignant tumours.

As for earthquakes, the earth's crust is constantly being reshaped by enormous tectonic forces underground, creating numerous ecological niches in which distinct and diverse forms of life may emerge. Heat produced by the decay of radioactive elements within the earth causes slowly moving convection currents in the earth's mantle (another non-linear dynamic process). New oceanic crust is formed at mid-ocean ridges and plunges back into the mantle. The descending slabs of oceanic crust become strained and fracture, causing

---

51. See, among numerous other works, John Polkinghorne, *Science and Providence* (London: SPCK, 1989); *The Faith of a Physicist: Reflections of a Bottom-Up Thinker, The Gifford Lectures, 1993–4* (Minneapolis, MN: Fortress, 1996).

earthquakes. Mountain ranges such as the Himalayas are formed when continents collide.

Thus earthquakes, volcanic eruptions and other awesome natural events are not aspects of "the fall," as has been understood in much of the Christian tradition, but rather are the way God has chosen to bring about ecological changes and biodiversity on the planet. The "fallenness" of the human condition is expressed in our increased vulnerability to such events. I have given examples above of how it is sinful human actions (including wrong priorities) that result in the heavy loss of life, much of which is preventable. Also, could we have, as a result of our fallenness, lost some capacities, such as immunity to deadly viruses and the ability to pick up nature's signals? (Some animals are able to sense seismic vibrations and approaching tsunamis and flee for safety.) We can only speculate on the possibilities.

I agree with David Fergusson's assessment that "there is at least a grain of truth in deism which requires acknowledgment." Instead of viewing every single event as if it were God acting in nature towards a specific end, deists "insisted upon a providence that worked in and through the regularities and contingencies of the world, even when this resulted in accident, mishap and tragedy. In loosening the fit between divine intention and created particularities, deism offered greater scope for freedom and contingency within the created order. Without committing wholesale to deism, we might acknowledge this."[52]

Also, if the cross of Christ is our guide to the way we think of the wisdom of God, then that wisdom is seen supremely in the bearing of the brokenness and alienation of the world. It is this that distinguishes the God of the biblical narrative from other gods. God remains omnipotent in the sense that he can do whatever he wills, but it seems not to be in accordance with his will to insist on total control. We have observed that the "control" model of divine sovereignty is inadequate to do full justice to the whole biblical picture.

Moreover, by endowing his creation with the power of true becoming, God indwells the temporality of God's creation. The Bible discloses God's identity through an unfolding narrative: a history of divine actions and responses. God makes room for the response and cooperation of created humanity. This is why the dominant note in the Scriptures seems to be one of God making *promises* for the future, rather than giving exact, detailed predictions of the future. Can we say the same for the created non-human world?

These are theologically controversial waters in which we are treading. God's relationship with his creation is *sui generis*, and his relationship with

52. Fergusson, *Providence of God*, 131–132.

time unknowable. But, along with some modern Christian theologians and philosophers, I would say, tentatively, that there is a sense in which we may say that God is "surprised" by the actualization of some events in the world even as he remains the ontological ground and source (Creator) of all that is.[53]

If the future is truly future, not yet there to be known, then it is no imperfection in God to say that he does not know the future. God knows perfectly the past *as past*, and he knows perfectly the future *as future*. God knows all the possible outcomes of free actions and free processes, but God knows them as possibilities until a particular outcome is actualized. God knows certainties as certainties and contingencies as contingent. Just as an artist embodies a purpose in her work and knows in outline what is going to be in it (and, in this sense, "foreknows" the end from the beginning), yet the material she works with (the feel of the brushes, the texture of the canvas, the density of the paint) contributes to the final product in its actuality, so God has a real future because of his freely chosen partnership with the created temporal world.

Finally, when tragedies such as earthquakes and hurricanes strike, the first thing to do is to express our human solidarity with the victims. There will follow, inevitably, the clamouring existential questions and our feeble, stuttering human answers. But more importantly, what we should experience is "a sense of *indignation* that 'the same thing' always happens and 'the same people' always suffer"; and "a *yearning* for things to be different some day."[54]

Let me conclude with some words that I wrote in response to the Asian tsunami of 26 December 2004:[55] In answer to the oft-asked question, "Where was God on the morning of the 26th December 2004?," we can say, humbly yet boldly, that the Triune God of sacrificial love was present in the pain and terror of the victims, in the grief of the survivors, in the heroism of people who risked their lives to save others, in the anger and protest expressed against the vulnerability of the poor in a technologically rich world, and in the outpouring of global compassion and selfless giving in the spontaneous tidal wave of humanity that was as unstoppable as the waves that broke on South Asia's coasts.

---

53. For some biblical examples of God's "surprise," even "disappointment," see Jer 3:6–7, 19–20; Isa 5:1–5; Ezek 22:26–27, 30–31.

54. Sobrino, *Where Is God?*, 11.

55. https://atyourservice.arocha.org/en/tsunami-tragedy-where-was-god/.

Epilogue

The *Cantate Domino* issued by the Council of Florence in 1441 affirmed the goodness of nature because, as a creation, it is grounded in the goodness of God:

> Most strongly [the Church] believes, professes, and declares that the one true God, Father, Son, and Holy Spirit, is the creator of all things visible and invisible, who, when He wished, out of His goodness created all creatures, spiritual as well as corporal; good, indeed, since they were made by the highest good, but changeable, since they were from nothing, and it asserts that nature is not evil since all nature, in so far as it is nature, is good.[56]

Leap forward to the early years of the twentieth century and the complaint of the prominent theosophist Annie Besant, who had a profound influence on the urban middle class in India and the nascent Indian struggle for independence: "I do not believe in God. My mind finds no grounds on which to build up a reasonable faith. My heart revolts against the spectre of an Almighty Indifference to the pain of sentient beings. My conscience rebels against the injustice, the cruelty, the inequality, which surround me on every side. But I believe in Man. In man's redeeming power; in man's re-moulding energy; in man's approaching triumph, through knowledge, love, and work."[57]

How ironic that Besant should glorify Man, when all the injustices and cruelties she bemoans are human, not divine, deeds. Not long after she wrote these words, Europe and the world were plunged into a senseless, barbaric war that sealed the coffin on the myth of Progress. And had she lived much longer into the twentieth century, she would have witnessed both human carnage and animal slaughter on a scale perhaps unprecedented in human history. She died the same year that Hitler came to power, and those who planned and implemented the Holocaust came from the most advanced scientific and artistic nation of the time. As Alister McGrath notes, they were "precisely those whom Ludwig Feuerbach declared to be the 'new gods' of the modern era, free from any divine prohibitions or sanctions, or any fear of future divine judgment." While many today, like Besant in an earlier age, affirm a belief in Humanity in preference to a belief in God, it is this humanity that "has been responsible for a series of moral, social, and political catastrophes, some

56. "The Council of Florence (A.D. 1438–1445) from Cantate Domino – Papal Bull of Pope Eugene IV," Catholicism.org, 16 March 2005.

57. Annie Besant, *Why I Do Not Believe in God* (1887), quoted in Alister McGrath, *The Twilight of Atheism: The Rise and Fall of Disbelief in the Modern World* (London: Rider, 2004), 183.

inspired by a belief in God, others by a belief that God must be eliminated, by all means and at all costs. The common denominator here is humanity, not divinity."[58]

Therefore, in the midst of all our agonies over unwarranted suffering and the apparent absence of God, we need to remember that, in the biblical perspective, it is human sin that is the great evil and from which flow all the other kinds of evil and misery. And so we return to the mystery of a suffering love that takes into its heart all the alienation and havoc that human sin wreaks on God's good world, and yet emerges triumphant. Philip Yancey tells the story of a Scottish woman named Margaret, stricken with throat cancer, who had a succession of well-meaning visitors who came into her hospital room with sympathetic comments. Finding it difficult to speak, she wrote these words on a piece of scrap paper: "This is not the worst thing to ever happen! Cancer is so limited. It cannot cripple love, shatter hope, corrode faith, eat away peace, destroy confidence, kill friendship, shut out memories, silence courage, quench the Spirit or lessen the power of Jesus."[59]

58. McGrath, *Twilight of Atheism*, 183–184.

59. Philip Yancey, *The Question That Never Goes Away* (Grand Rapids, MI: Zondervan, 2013), 104.

5

The Future Tense

Sarah's laughter is faith's constant companion.[1]

We have seen how the embrace of suffering and death in the Trinitarian event of the crucifixion speaks, paradoxically, of the presence of God in God-forsakenness. Golgotha takes to its uttermost the holy love of God in its encounter with violence and the hostile, alienating power of death. In the dying and death of Jesus, the Triune God suffers dying and death, but is not dead. In choosing to suffer death both with us and at our hands, out of his desire for our reconciliation, God overcomes death. That is the victory witnessed to in the resurrection of Jesus from among the dead. God continues to participate in the death of all human beings, but the "sting" of death has been decisively removed in the death experienced on Golgotha.[2] But this central truth of the gospel has often been deformed by Christians eager to present the resurrection of Jesus as a *reversal* of the cross, a cancellation, a magic "answer" to suffering, disability and the end to all human limits. The resurrection is then either deployed solely as an apologetic argument or else to serve a triumphalist ideology of health and worldly success.

1. Ernst Käsemann, *Perspectives on Paul* (1971), cited in David Fergusson, *The Providence of God: A Polyphonic Approach* (Cambridge: Cambridge University Press, 2018), 297. The reference is to Sarah's incredulous laughter as she overhears the divine promise to Abraham that she will bear a son despite her age (Gen 18:12). When Isaac is born she laughs again, but this time with joy; and she goes further, declaring that everyone who hears about this miraculous event will laugh too (Gen 22:6). Hence Sarah's laughter signifies two kinds of human disbelief – that of doubt and of uncomprehending joy. It is the first that Käsemann refers to. It is part of the argument of this book that the second can only emerge after an honest struggle with the first.

2. For atheistic naturalism, death is defined as non-being, biological disintegration. For the vast majority of religious humankind, death is not non-being but a transition to another mode of being. Either way, death is "experienced" as the ultimate dissolution of all relationships. In biblical thought, as we saw in ch. 3, what gives death its alienating "sting" is sin. The "wages of sin is death" (Rom 6:23).

The denouement of the resurrection *is* a reversal – of our human values and judgments. But it is better grasped as a *double vindication*. First, it is a vindication of who Jesus claimed to be. His claims offended the guardians of morals and religion and he was crucified as a blasphemer, a rebel against the empire, a messianic pretender.

> What the resurrection has told us about the man now laid before us in a cemetery, at the end of a life begun in a cowshed and concluded on a cross, is that this is God incarnate . . . What the good news of Easter does so stunningly to the Jesus story is confirm that after all, in this person who lived so humanly and with such inhumanity was put to death, we have been witnesses to heavenly love embodied and enacted.[3]

Second, it is a vindication of the path Jesus chose to tread. It is helpful to think of the cross as a crossroads, a conjunction of two paths. The first path is the way of Adam, wayward and alienated humanity, under the sway of evil powers. It is seen in the custodians of Israel's religious traditions who were furious at Jesus's provocative nonconformity and the outrageous claims he made; in the crowds who were enraged at his refusal to be the nationalist revolutionary they expected the Messiah to be; in the disciples' desire to be in positions of power, lording it over others; in Caiaphas, the high priest, whose pragmatic, utilitarian reasoning justified sacrificing innocent victims in order to protect his privileged autonomy vis-à-vis the imperial power; and in Pilate, the representative of the latter, who hungered for popularity with Caesar and the people of Judea, and so was indifferent to matters of truth or justice.

The other path is the way taken by Jesus, the last Adam. It's seen in his steadfast commitment to what he understood as his vocation, showing his people what it meant to be Israel – the "covenant community" of Yahweh and a "light to the nations"; in his practice of humble servanthood as he befriends the "dregs" of society; in his scorn for popularity and reputation; in his selfless loving of the poor and helpless; in his confrontation of moral and religious hypocrisy, and the tears he sheds over the sacred city; in his refusal to return evil with evil, and instead to offer forgiveness and reconciliation even to his

---

3. Alan E. Lewis, *Between Cross and Resurrection: A Theology of Holy Saturday* (Grand Rapids, MI: Eerdmans, 2001), 80–81. Lewis highlights the "chilling" corollary of this: "that he in whom God dwelled, who did his Father's will and revealed his Father's face, now lies still in the pose of death, abandoned and defeated. God's absence and the tomb's cold godlessness, which seemed so frightening when the grave itself had seemed to prove that it did *not* contain the Son of God, is now a thousand times more chilling when Easter exaltation has assured us that the Son of God is precisely whom the grave contains" (83).

(and his nation's) enemies; in his refusal to let his disciples fight for him or to summon angels to defend himself; in the agony he experienced in Gethsemane as he struggled with the full implications of his filial vocation; and, finally, as he dies as yet another of the despised and dehumanized victims of the imperial Pax Romana.

Here we have two roads which meet at the cross: two radically different attitudes to life, two radically different understandings of what faith in the reign of God the Creator entails. There are many people today who confidently tell us that the way of Jesus is the way of weaklings. If we really want to get ahead in life, we must assert ourselves, be simply pragmatic and utilitarian in our thinking. The end justifies the means, whether in one's personal life or in business and politics. Think first of your own safety and well-being. Give up all those idealistic dreams of putting the world to rights, all that childish talk of "moral principles" and "obedience to God" – that's the way of immature cowards. It's also the sure way to failure.

Now, if Jesus had died and that was the end of him, we would have to admit that these sceptics are right. Obeying Jesus is a lost cause. But the resurrection of Jesus tells us that it is the way of Jesus that is the only way to be truly alive. The resurrection proves that it is the way of sacrificial love, of total obedience to God and patient endurance in the midst of suffering, that eventually will bring forth the kingdom of God's justice and peace. It is the resurrection that assures us that it is Jesus's way of living and dying that will ultimately triumph.

But that is not all. Jesus does not divest himself of our humanity in his resurrection, but in the ascension takes our human nature, healed and transfigured, into the very heart of God for ever.

I mentioned in chapter 3 Karl Barth's innovative assertion that in Christ's suffering, death and resurrection, God descends and humanity is raised. His death was a *divine* happening and his exaltation a *human* happening. Moreover, human bodies are more than biological machines. They are fundamental to our unique personal identities, the vehicles by which we enter into and maintain social relationships. Bodies make it possible for us to know others and for others to know us. So, proclaiming the bodily resurrection of Jesus as the "firstfruits" of the resurrection of the dead is to say not only that the world to come will be, like this one, made of physical stuff (albeit transformed in ways that we cannot now comprehend), but that it will also be profoundly social, a communal sharing in the Trinitarian life of God.

The Christian gospel is precisely about the Triune God bringing about something *astonishingly new*, something which is not merely a development of the inherent potentialities and possibilities of the historical present. This is where Christian hope departs from mere secular futurology – attempts to track historical and social trends and so predict what is to come. Christian hope rests not upon our capacities or the capacities of the present creation but upon the action of the creator God who summons forth life out of death in the resurrection of Jesus Christ. This is an action in which faith discerns both an anticipation and a pledge of the ultimate renewal of all things. As Oliver O'Donovan remarks, "The Christ-event, though accomplished, is still an event for the future, and our faith in it must still be marked by a hope, and not a hope for our own private futures only but for the future of the world subject to God's reign."[4]

Hope as Struggle

"Judaism," according to Rabbi Jonathan Sacks, "is faith in the future tense." He points to four remarkable and related ideas: a God whose name is in the future tense, a future-oriented concept of time, a literature whose stories always end in a future-not-yet-reached, and a golden age which belongs to the future. This contrasts with the Greek "tragic view of life" where even the greatest heroes cannot escape their destiny or fate. Where there is only history and no freedom, there is no hope. Where there is history and freedom, there is hope. And where there is hope, there are disasters but no ultimate tragedy. Sacks concludes, "Jews were and are still called on to be the voice of hope in the conversation of humankind."[5]

The prophetic tradition disrupts the cycles of excessive optimism and disillusionment that are a familiar feature of many societies. It asserts the goodness of life without denying the evidence that would justify despair. Thus "Hebrew spirituality," the American political theologian Reinhold Niebuhr (1892–1971) asserted, "was never corrupted by either the optimism which conceived the world as possessing unqualified sanctity and goodness or the pessimism which relegated historic existence to a realm of meaningless cycles."[6]

The early church, even as it rapidly became predominantly Gentile, took as their Scriptures the Bible of the Jews and so inherited this future tense from Judaism. Indeed, hope sums up what is unique about the biblical story:

4. Oliver O'Donovan, *The Desire of the Nations: Rediscovering the Roots of Political Theology* (Cambridge: Cambridge University Press, 1996), 144.

5. Jonathan Sacks, *Future Tense: A Vision for Jews and Judaism in the Global Culture* (London: Hodder & Stoughton, 2009), 241, 252.

6. Quoted in Christopher Lasch, *The True and Only Heaven: Progress and Its Critics* (New York: W. W. Norton, 1991), 373.

living towards the future, not nostalgic longing for the past (no "golden age") nor believing that freedom and responsibility are illusions. The writer of the New Testament Epistle to the Hebrews sums up the faith of the patriarchs and prophets of Israel this way: "All these people were still living by faith when they died. They did not receive the things promised; they only saw them and welcomed them from a distance . . . If they had been thinking of the country they had left, they would have had opportunity to return. Instead, they were longing for a better country – a heavenly one. Therefore God is not ashamed to be called their God, for he has prepared a city for them" (Heb 11:13, 15–16).

The seer of Revelation takes the imagery of a future city further. The biblical story that begins with a couple cultivating a garden ends in a city coming down from heaven to fill the earth. This is a multicultural city, drawing together people of all languages and cultures. The gates of the city stand open to receive the "glory and honour of the nations" (Rev 21:24, 26): all the cultural wealth of the earth, the products of human labour. Salvation includes the final gathering up into the all-embracing worship of God all that is truly human in all places and at all times, those human acts that reflect the beauty, love, justice and truth of God.

But, of course, where Christianity parts company from Judaism is in its foundational conviction that God's promised future has already dawned in the resurrection of Jesus the Messiah. The evil that has disfigured God's good creation has been decisively defeated. Incredible as this may seem in the light of the indescribable evils that continue to be unleashed upon the earth and all its creatures by human beings and the institutions they create, nevertheless Christians hold to this conviction, based not on wishful thinking or naïveté but on divine promise and historical event. Indeed, as the Sri Lankan ecumenical statesman Daniel Thambyrajah Niles (1908–70) profoundly expressed it, "Hope begins with the ruin of our expectations."

Lesslie Newbigin, former Bishop of Madras in India and another of the twentieth century's great ecumenical statesmen, once spoke of "a faith that rebels and a faith that accepts." These, he said, always belong together. Jesus consistently attacked the powers of evil, whether in the sicknesses that afflicted the body and soul, the exclusion of poverty and handicap, the hypocrisy of religious leaders, or the exploitation and oppression of social practices and conventions.

> He sent out his disciples to do the same. And yet he also told them that they must of necessity suffer, just as he would have to suffer. This paradox is at the very heart of the Gospel: "He saved others,

> himself he cannot save." It belongs to the mission of the church to the end. The power given to the church to meet the power of evil is just the power to follow Jesus on the road that leads through suffering, through total surrender to the Father, to the gift of new life and a new world.[7]

But not all the sick in Galilee and Judaea were healed, not all the dead raised, not all injustice reversed. The kingdom of God, inaugurated by Jesus, is both now and not yet, here and not here. This is important to remember, not least because the healing miracles of Jesus and his apostles are sometimes wielded against the sick and those with disabilities as if their alleged lack of faith is what is preventing them from experiencing full health. Even within the pages of the New Testament, we read that Paul had to learn to live with his mysterious impairment (his "thorn in the flesh," 2 Cor 12:7–9) on top of all his other hardships because God's "power is made perfect in weakness."

The theologian Nancy Eiesland has written how she found in the crucified and risen Jesus a radically different perspective on, rather than a "solution" to, her own disability:

> In presenting his impaired hands and feet to his startled friends, the resurrected Jesus is revealed as the disabled God. Jesus, the resurrected saviour, calls for his frightened companions to recognize in the marks of impairment their own connection with God, their own salvation. In so doing, this disabled God is also the revealer of a new humanity. The disabled God is not only the one from heaven but the revelation of true personhood, underscoring the reality that full personhood is fully compatible with the experience of disability.[8]

The earthly wounds that the resurrected Christ showed his disciples can, in the opinion of artist and art teacher Bruce Herman, become the basis of a new aesthetic – a "broken beauty" – and "a means of working through and beyond pain to a perfection that need not participate in the idealized, unattainable standards of our celebrity and youth-obsessed culture."[9] Such beauty can be found in the aged and infirm no less than in youthful, healthy figures, but such

---

7. Lesslie Newbigin, *The Open Secret* (London: SPCK, 1978), 121.

8. Nancy Eiesland, *The Disabled God: Towards a Liberatory Theology of Disability* (Nashville: Abingdon Press, 1994), 100.

9. Bruce Herman, "Wounds and Beauty," in *The Beauty of God: Theology and the Arts*, ed. Daniel J. Treier, Mark Husbands and Roger Lundin (Downers Grove, IL: IVP Academic, 2007), 111.

a discovery requires many years of committed love. Herman's thesis is summed up as follows: "Only eyes trained by gazing continually toward the cross – only eyes cleansed by that second innocence, childlike habitual clarity – can see true beauty, true goodness."[10] Van Gogh said he could not look at the portraits of ordinary people by Rembrandt without believing in God.[11]

In the last few months of my wife Karin's terminal illness, we often returned to two of our favourite biblical texts: Romans 8 and 2 Corinthians 4. What is common to both is the interweaving of the themes of "suffering" and "glory." In Romans 8, Paul speaks of three "groanings." There are those of the totality of creation ("groaning as in the pains of childbirth," v. 22), awaiting eagerly its liberation from bondage to corruptibility and the revelation of the new humanity with whose future the creation is indissolubly linked. There are the groans of those who belong to the new creation already, the adopted sons and daughters of God, who "groan inwardly" as they await their full redemption (v. 23). And there is the solidarity of the Holy Spirit with us and the rest of God's creation, "[interceding] for us through wordless groans" (v. 26). Clearly, groaning with longing is the language of hope. For "hope that is seen is no hope at all. Who hopes for what they already have?" (v. 24). This is, after all, authentic prayer – in the moving words of Alan Lewis, "desperation translated into daring." Post-Easter prayer is to "confess not the abundance but the exhaustion of one's verbal, intellectual, and spiritual resources. It is surrender to one who prays for us when we have no prayers left and can do so only when we acknowledge our bankruptcy of spirit."[12]

Paul, then, knew – with an intensity we rarely attain – what it means to struggle in hope, to live in the tension between the "now" and the "not yet." He uses the childbirth metaphor again when describing his own ministry among the Galatians (Gal 4:19), reminding them how he was struggling with illness when he first preached to them (4:13), and now feared that his labour among them had been wasted (4:11). In his letter to the Romans, he speaks of his "great sorrow and unceasing anguish" over the unbelief of his fellow Jews and wishes that he might even be "cursed and cut off from Christ" for their sake (Rom 9:2–3). And we know that his missionary desire to reach beyond Rome to Spain, the boundary of civilization as then understood, was frustrated by the squabbles within the churches he had planted and the imprisonment he eventually experienced in Rome because of his own countrymen.

---

10. Herman, "Wounds and Beauty," 119.

11. Richard Harries, *Art and the Beauty of God* (London/New York: Continuum, 1993), 132.

12. Lewis, *Between Cross and Resurrection*, 64.

It is in his (canonical) second letter to the Corinthians, the most deeply personal of all his letters, that the heart of the apostle is disclosed most movingly. He begins by reminding them of the troubles he and his companions experienced in the province of Asia. "We were under great pressure, far beyond our ability to endure, so that we despaired of life itself. Indeed, we felt we had received the sentence of death" (2 Cor 1:8–9). Towards the end of his letter he lists a catalogue of personal humiliations and physical suffering (11:23–29), and tosses off, almost as a parenthesis, the "daily . . . pressure of my concern for all the churches" (11:28).

But it is in the great missionary fourth chapter that we encounter the most poignant expression of what we may call Paul's "eschatological heart":

> But we have this treasure [the gospel] in jars of clay to show that this all-surpassing power is from God and not from us. We are hard pressed on every side, but not crushed; perplexed, but not in despair; persecuted, but not abandoned; struck down, but not destroyed. We always carry around in our body the death of Jesus, so that the life of Jesus may also be revealed in our body. For we who are alive are always being given over to death for Jesus' sake, so that his life may also be revealed in our mortal body. So then, death is at work in us, but life is at work in you. (2 Cor 4:7–12)

Ever since the church's first great conflict with the power of imperial Rome, the victory of the gospel has been won not by the efficiency of its management programmes, the sophistication of its theologies or the cleverness of its preachers, but by the blood of its martyrs. This simple yet profound truth – that the authenticating marks of Christian mission (as opposed to mere proselytization, social work or religious propaganda) are the marks of suffering – has been much neglected in the missiology emanating from the theological centres of the past two hundred years. Yet it is intriguing that whenever Paul's claim to be an authentic apostle of Jesus was questioned, his reply was always to describe his share in the sufferings of Christ.[13]

The church suffers when it lives as a counter-community, calling into question the dominant values and ideologies that maintain the status quo. Also, when it openly identifies with the weak and vulnerable members of society, victims of those dominant values and ideologies, whether they be laissez-faire capitalism, communism, fascism, racism, nationalism or patriarchy. A church which like the priest and the Levite in Jesus's parable of the good Samaritan

13. Cf. 1 Cor 4:8–13; 2 Cor 4; 5; 12:1–10; Gal 6:14–17; Col 1:24; Eph 3:13.

passes by on the other side is not the church understood as the body of Christ. "Suffering is what makes the church authentic," observes Raymond Fung of Hong Kong. "If the church is to be the church, it must have the marks of Jesus Christ upon it – the marks of the beatings, the nails, and the crown of thorns – the signs of the cross. With these marks, the church becomes authentic not only before God, but also before those who suffer, people who are sinned against."[14]

This sort of thinking does not feature in the understanding of missionary "success" and the methodologies for church growth that abound in "evangelical" circles today. Christian mission is not a success story in the way the world reckons success; and the outstanding examples of vibrant Christian witness in recent times have been in places where Christian flourishing was least expected: in China, for instance, where the church has emerged from the horrors of the Cultural Revolution and sporadic waves of repression greatly renewed and strengthened; in Eastern Europe, where the courage and holiness of Christian lives continued to attract people to the gospel, despite attempts by powerful governments to stamp it out; and in Latin America, where despotic right-wing governments have imprisoned and tortured to death countless believers.

But, lest we think that the newer churches of the Majority World are immune from the betrayals of the gospel that are often associated with European Christendom and large swathes of North American suburban Christianity, we need only look at the disastrous fragmentation and competitive rivalry among churches, the authoritarian forms of leadership that are emerging everywhere, and Christian politicians and pastors who have thrown in their lot with brutal dictators and xenophobic demagogues. We need only recall recent examples of racist and tribal violence committed by "born-again" Protestants and Roman Catholics in countries such as Rwanda and Burundi, not very different from Nazi supporters in the German Lutheran church of the 1930s or white supremacists in the American "Bible Belt."

In his monumental volume *Christianity in the Twentieth Century*, historian Brian Stanley, while recognizing that "racial hatred" is not the best terminology to deploy in describing many of the twentieth-century's genocidal acts, whether in Turkey in 1915–16, Nazi Germany, or Rwanda and Burundi in 1994, asserts that it is "undeniable" that churches in many instances proved receptive to racist ideologies, and this poses "uncomfortable questions for Christian theology." He points out that the profession of Christian belief or even the possession

14. Raymond Fung, "Evangelism Today," in *Living Theology in Asia*, ed. John England (London: SCM, 1981), 80.

of theological qualifications did not provide "an effective firewall against the virus of ethnic hostility"; and he bemoans the fact that

> For Christians, what is doubly disturbing about the unprecedented scale and rate of ethnic killing in these . . . cases is the seeming impotence of their faith to resist the destructive power of racial hatred. The two holocausts – in Nazi Germany and in Rwanda – . . . tell a depressing story of widespread, though never total, capitulation by churches and Christian leaders to the insidious attractions of racial ideology, and of the habitual silence or inaction of many Christians in the face of observed atrocities.[15]

Similarly, in the context of the apartheid era, Manas Buthelezi, a South African Lutheran bishop, lamented that "The ecclesiastical umbrella of confessions and of teaching has been lamentably ineffective against the storms of racism."[16] Stanley ends by cautioning the church about invoking simplistic appeals for justice, as such rhetoric is readily hijacked in the interests of ethnic or nationalist interests. He quotes the late Roman Catholic historian of the African church Adrian Hastings, who commented on the Bosnian genocide of 1993, but with earlier German examples in mind, that "Without a very strong sense of the power of sin, of evil in the world, it is impossible to formulate a theology of politics or of history, or to defend the ground out of which effective prophecy can come."[17] It is this awareness of the depths of sin in human affairs that should lead Christians to continual self-criticism and repentance, before censuring others.

Hope as Vulnerable Action

When Paul receives the response "my power is made perfect in weakness" (2 Cor 12:9) to his thrice-repeated prayer for deliverance, we are invited to enlarge our imagination when it comes to both discerning God's action in history and shaping our own. We tend to think of power as the use of force or aggressive action to bend the wills of others to our own. But power is also exercised through inspiring, influencing or persuading people to change their attitudes, allegiances and intellectual horizons. This is the way of creative artists

---

15. Brian Stanley, *Christianity in the Twentieth Century: A World History* (Princeton, NJ: Princeton University Press, 2018), 151, 153–154.

16. Quoted in John Parratt, *Reinventing Christianity: African Theology Today* (Grand Rapids, MI: Eerdmans; Trenton, NJ: Africa World Press, 1995), 169.

17. Stanley, *Christianity in the Twentieth Century*, 171.

and social visionaries; and this seems to be the primary, if not exclusive, way[18] the power of a suffering God works in his world.

The power of vulnerability is also experienced in our relationships with little children and with adults with severe disabilities. I have seen hulking giants dissolve in floods of tears as they cradle newborn infants in their arms, infants they could easily crush to death with a mere flexing of their fingers. I referred in a previous chapter to the L'Arche communities which bring together volunteer carers and adults with learning disabilities. Henri Nouwen, who left his Harvard professorship to be such a volunteer, wrote of his life-transforming encounter with Adam, the man who was given to his care:

> After a month of working with Adam, something started to happen to me that had never happened to me before. This deeply handicapped young man, who by many outsiders is considered an embarrassment, a distortion of humanity, a useless creature who should not have been allowed to be born, started to become my dearest companion. As my fears gradually decreased, a love started to emerge in me so full of tenderness and affection that most of my other tasks seemed boring and superficial compared with the hours spent with Adam. Out of this broken body and broken mind emerged a most beautiful human being offering me a greater gift than I could ever be able to offer him. It is hard for me to find adequate words for this experience, but somehow Adam revealed to me who he was and who I was and how we can love each other . . . The longer I stayed with Adam the more clearly I started to see him as my gentle teacher, teaching me what no book, school or professor could ever have taught me.[19]

This power of the weak, freely chosen by a God who allows suffering to befall him, to be affected by his creation and to take its finitude into his infinite being, is, of course, the antithesis of modern secular notions of power. Not to be in control, to submit to limits not of our choice: that is our greatest fear. And it is understandable when we recognize how autonomy has been

18. I say primary but not exclusive because God does work coercively through political and judicial authorities; and also by way of "miracles" which, however exceptional in God's providential ordering of his creation, nevertheless do happen. Here I differ from Process Theology, which only has room for a divine "luring" or "persuasive influence," as well as from Dietrich Bonhoeffer and Paul Fiddes, whose writings have exercised a deep influence (even if not coercive!) on me.

19. Henri Nouwen, "Adam's Story: The Peace That Is Not of This World," *Weavings*, Mar–Apr 1988.

wrested out of the hands of women, the sick, the elderly, the poor and ethnic minorities throughout human history in ways that have permanently damaged them and also the ones who have wielded such control. But autonomy can be absolutized in equally damaging ways. Dissatisfied with our fragile humanity, we want to master every process from reproduction to our dying. We fear ageing and its attendant dependence, and those who can afford it desperately clutch at every medical promise of a life-expanding elixir or a digital longevity in virtual reality.

And yet, as the bioethicist Gilbert Meilaender observes:

> It is aging that keeps us from imagining that everything our hearts desire could be given through more of the same kind of life. And it is aging, wearing down, that enables us to cultivate within ourselves the capacity for self-giving and self-sacrifice that makes place for those who come after us. To grow old, to wear down, even to die – and to know and acknowledge this as part of life's trajectory – is fitting for a creature who is neither beast nor god, and whose dignity consists in being human.[20]

Furthermore, he notes elsewhere that "To live an indefinitely prolonged life but never to see God, to be always on the way but with no *telos* that gives a point to the journey, might be pleasant in many ways, but it could not satisfy the heart's deepest desire."[21]

Of course, Christian theology nurtures an ambivalent attitude to death. It is a natural limit that God places on life to enable other generations to take our place. But death can never be truly "natural" for humans, precisely because, unlike other animals who die, humans are conscious of it, and that consciousness makes it also unnatural. It is the destroyer of relationships and of meaning without which humans find it impossible to be human. For we are social beings who live by the future tense. We entertain a horizon of possibilities that cannot be contained within the limits of nature. We make plans, embark on projects, and cultivate expectations and ambitions that far exceed our temporal moment. When death arrives, therefore, especially when suddenly but also late in life, it comes as the interruption of an unfinished story.

> When someone we love dies, we feel more than shock and deprivation. We feel outraged, resentful. We feel that a kind of

---

20. Gilbert Meilaender, *Neither Beast Nor God* (New York: Encounter Books, 2009), 73.

21. Gilbert Meilaender, *Should We Live Forever? The Ethical Ambiguities of Aging* (Grand Rapids, MI: Eerdmans, 2013), 51.

> injustice has been done . . . We have a life-story because by our own decisions we make something of the life we receive . . . when another animal dies at the hand of nature, nature is simply taking back what she has lent. But when we die at the hands of nature, nature is a usurer taking away more than we received from her. Hence our sense of outrage and injustice.[22]

Thus, the Christian ambivalence in the face of death. When people die young, through an act of violence, accident or sickness, it is right to be angry. But this was normal for most of our recorded history, and still is the norm in many parts of the Majority World. As Montaigne wrote, observing his sixteenth-century society, "To die of age is a rare, singular, and extraordinary death, and so much less natural than others: it is the last and extremest kind of dying."[23] And Alan Lewis, in his remarkable book *Between Cross and Resurrection: A Theology of Holy Saturday* which he completed during the last stages of terminal cancer, commented: "How foolish and hollow sound the protests of the healthy and the wealthy and the safe, against the unjust shortness of their lives, when heard against the cries of those who hopelessly endure the banal monotony of evil, unending cycles of poverty and famine, war, oppression and abuse, and for whom the shortening of life would be good news indeed."[24]

Lewis goes on to remind us that

> Our tears are but the slightest drop in the ocean of God's own weeping over young lives brutally curtailed, and old extended beyond all meaning, in pain, indignity, and helplessness. The Friday wail of Christ's forsakenness, and his descent into hell on Saturday, provide our final reassurance that God cries out with us in our abandonment in the tyranny of evil, and will go to any lengths that all things and all persons might be delivered from captivity to death.[25]

Without denying the uniqueness of Christ's agony, we may still learn from Christ in Gethsemane that, in the face of death, it is fitting to lament, to cry out to God, to ask that we be spared death. We may also learn from Christ to

22. Herbert McCabe, "Life after Death," in *The McCabe Reader*, ed. Brian Davies and Paul Kucharski (London: Bloomsbury T&T Clark, 2016), 354–355.

23. Cited in Atul Gawande, *Being Mortal: Illness, Medicine, and What Matters in the End* (London: Profile, 2014), 32.

24. Lewis, *Between Cross and Resurrection*, 415.

25. Lewis, 426.

trust the one who will finally save us, not necessarily from a premature death nor even from its fear, but finally from the power of death. And, when a loved one dies, it is also fitting that we grieve and lament, because we have come face to face with the last enemy. However much we may believe in the final resurrection, we have suffered a genuine loss that is irreplaceable. Sadness must be allowed to do its cleansing work. "There is a Yiddish proverb that calls tears the soap of the soul. The release, rather than the bottling up, of inarticulate emotion is a valuable first aid to be applied over and over again to the raw wounds of grief."[26] In Shakespeare's *Macbeth* the bereaved Macduff is told, "Give sorrow words. The grief that does not speak / Whispers the o'er-fraught heart, and bids it break."[27]

Grief is a universal human experience; and yet every experience of grief is unique. How we grieve – and for how long – depends on many factors, such as how close the relationship was with the one we have lost; whether death came suddenly and unexpectedly, or was a long-drawn-out affair; whether we harbour feelings of regret or remorse; how we have been brought up to deal with our emotions; and cultural practices and expectations. Also, it can never be hurried. Every experience of grief has its own timetable; its pace must be respected, and not determined by those who do not share in the grief.

Reading accounts of grief by the more articulate and reflective amongst us can enable us to recognize our own feelings and clarify our own internal conversations. William Abraham, an American philosopher and theologian, wrote after the loss of his son (in his twenties):

> Words fail us; we are too traumatized to speak; we simply have to sit or walk around or hold our heads in our hands and live with our piercing pain, our tears, our sobs, and our silences. We have to do what we can to find a way to get up and go on, to secure strategies of survival and negotiation when speech itself fails us . . . What happens in this instance is the breakdown of our normal cognitive capacities. The darkness has snuffed out the light by which we engage in reason insofar as it relates to the excruciating loss involved.[28]

26. Leslie C. Allen, *A Liturgy of Grief: A Pastoral Commentary on Lamentations* (Grand Rapids, MI: Baker Academic, 2011), 2.

27. William Shakespeare, *Macbeth*, Act 4, Scene 3.

28. William J. Abraham, *Among the Ashes: On Death, Grief, and Hope* (Grand Rapids, MI: Eerdmans, 2017), 14–15.

Can grief be creative? Once again, we take our bearings from the cross. The Triune God, as the ultimate victim, bears the full brunt of sin and evil in order to create a new situation for creatures like us who are held in bondage by the power of sin and evil. Forgiveness is a creative act, for the victim invites the offender to refuse to remain mired in the past but to embark on a new journey. It offers to wipe the slate clean, to begin anew. And because forgiveness has reconciliation as its ultimate aim, the response of the offender is vital. Even in our human acts of forgiveness, as we absorb the pain done to us by the offender and refuse to demand our "right" to retaliation, the relationship is mended when the offender is moved by our offer of forgiveness to admit the offence and to receive what is freely offered. Then follows whatever restitution may be required, depending on the circumstances. But restitution or compensation is not first demanded as a condition of forgiveness. Nevertheless, forgiveness effects reconciliation only when received as well as offered. If rejected, the relationship remains unmended. Such forgiveness, which labels evil as evil but does not return evil with evil, has a creative power, in both personal and political contexts.

Grief can also be creative in so far as it opens up conversations with people about the reality of death, a topic that is taboo in many so-called developed countries. Jerry Sittser writes about his grief following the death of his wife and children in a road accident: "I realized soon after the accident that I had another significant responsibility to fulfil too, and that concerned my role in the community as an interpreter of my experience. Friends wanted to listen and empathize; but they also wanted to learn, to reflect on the universal nature of suffering, and to make meaning for their own lives. So we became a reflective community together."[29]

Sharing in God's own protest against unjust suffering should also lead to our turning away from indulgent self-pity and the temptation to nurse feelings of resentment against others, to actions in the world that address the causes of unjust suffering and needless deaths. We can also create spaces in local communities for others to share their own stories of suffering which have largely been ignored, as, for instance, in the #MeToo movement, or (on a larger political stage) the various truth and reconciliation commissions that have been set up in countries in the aftermath of civil strife.

Yes, grief embitters many people and leaves its deep scars on others around them. "You can't see anything properly while your eyes are blurred with tears,"

29. Jerry Sittser, *A Grace Disguised* (Grand Rapids, MI: Zondervan, 2004), 182.

wrote C. S. Lewis after his wife Joy Davidman died of cancer.[30] This is why it is wise advice not to make far-reaching decisions when in a state of bereavement. But there are also many who will testify that grief has made them less self-centred, and more empathetic and compassionate. Not long after the death of his own son in a mountaineering accident, Nicholas Wolterstorff held out the realistic hope that "I shall [always] look at the world through tears. Perhaps I shall see things that dry-eyed I could not see." Wolterstorff went on to lay down a moving challenge both to himself and to others who struggle with their own pain: "If sympathy for the world's wounds is not enlarged by our anguish, if love for those around us is not expanded, if gratitude for what is good does not flame up, if insight is not deepened, if commitment to what is important is not strengthened, if aching for a new day is not intensified, if hope is weakened and faith diminished, if from the experience of death comes nothing good, then death has won. Then death, be proud."[31]

Hope as a Prophetic Way of Life

Christian hope is twofold: for God's reign within this present creation and for God's new creation. The distinction is customarily labelled proximate and ultimate hope. We yearn for liberation within this created order, especially liberation from injustice and God's protection of that created order from disfigurement; and we hope for that transformed mode of existence, glimpsed in the incarnate life and resurrection of Jesus, that heralds a new order, continuous with but also radically discontinuous with the present. Proximate hope depends not only on God but also on human actions. Hence it can, and does, always disappoint even as it brings about real progress. But ultimate hope depends purely on God's promised action, and that is why the apostle Paul calls it "a hope that does not disappoint" (Rom 5:5 NRSV).

What we do in the world is not a condition for the coming of God's kingdom. God's kingdom, on the contrary, is the condition for our acting; it underwrites the intelligibility of what we do.

God takes our actions – whether cultivating gardens, developing technologies, making poetry, composing music, designing cities, feeding the hungry – and, purging them from all taint of sin, re-inscribes them and their fruit within the life of his new creation. After a grave illness, poet-theologian John Donne (1572–1631) penned "Hymn to God, My God, in My Sickness" in

---

30. C. S. Lewis, *A Grief Observed* (London: Faber & Faber, 1961), 37.

31. Nicholas Wolterstorff, *Lament for a Son* (Grand Rapids, MI: Eerdmans, 1987), 26, 92.

which he pictured himself just outside heaven's door, tuning up to the sounds of the throng on the other side, just as a child might sneak into the back of an orchestral rehearsal and try tuning her instrument to the sounds of the great ensemble she hopes one day to join:

> Since I am coming to that holy room,
>   Where, with thy choir of saints for evermore,
> I shall be made thy music; as I come,
>   I tune the instrument here at the door,
>   And what I must do then, think here before.[32]

Images of the eschaton are given to us in Scripture, not to satisfy our curiosity or to invite idle speculation, but in order to transform our living in the present. The way God's Spirit does this is by capturing our imagination. Prophecy is essentially the gift of looking beyond the present which is defined for us by the ruling powers that be, and envisaging an alternative reality. The subversive character of Jesus's life and ministry was due to the fact that, in the words of Gustavo Gutiérrez, he saw "the utopia that sets history in motion."[33] He confronted the status quo, challenging what is in the name of what is to come. The kingdom of God was for him a vision that demanded costly praxis. Wherever we may happen to live, and whether we are struggling against oppressive regimes, political apathy, the ravaging of our natural habitats, financial corruption or sheer indifference, we require "a compelling vision that surpasses and so relativizes the contemporary moment, a vision that breaks our cultural hypnosis and moves us to hope for more than what we see, a vision that breeds impatience and keeps us ill-adjusted to so-called reality."[34]

It is fascinating to read contemporary secular socialists and Marxist intellectuals clinging to the notion of utopia and, indeed, explicitly messianic language, thus revealing the deep historical debt of Marxism to biblical (prophetic) ways of thought.[35] For instance, the American social critic Russell Jacoby laments the "end of utopia" and echoes Theodore Adorno's exhortation to "contemplate all things as they would present themselves from

---

32. John Donne, "Hymn to God, My God, in My Sickness," in *John Donne: The Major Works, Including Songs and Sonnets and Sermons*, cited in Jeremy Begbie, *Resounding Truth: Christian Wisdom in the World of Music* (London: SPCK, 2007), 308.

33. Gustavo Gutiérrez, *The God of Life* (1991), cited in Dale C. Allison, Jr., *Night Comes: Death, Imagination, and the Last Things* (Grand Rapids, MI: Eerdmans, 2016), 90.

34. Allison, *Night Comes*, 91.

35. I have discussed this connection in chapter 4 of my *Gods That Fail: Modern Idolatry and Christian Mission* (1996; 2nd ed., Eugene, OR: Wipf & Stock, 2016).

the standpoint of redemption" (or view the world "as it will appear one day in the messianic light").[36] Jacoby explains that in an "era of political resignation and fatigue the utopian spirit remains more necessary than ever. It evokes neither prisons nor programs, but an idea of human solidarity and happiness." The world, says Jacoby, has turned cold and grey because it has been stripped of anticipation. What is to be done? "Nothing is to be done. Yet that does not mean nothing is to be thought or imagined or dreamed. On the contrary. The effort to envision other possibilities of life and society remains urgent and constitutes the essential precondition for doing something."[37]

Crossing the Atlantic, we meet the Irish literary theorist Terry Eagleton who, while unashamedly defending Christianity against the new atheists, professes to be an atheist Marxist himself.

> Why, then, do some of us still cling to this political faith [socialism] in the teeth of what many would regard as reason and solid evidence? Not only, I think, because socialism is such an extraordinarily good idea that it has proved exceedingly hard to discredit, and this despite its own most strenuous efforts. It is also because one cannot accept that this – the world we see groaning in agony around us – is the only way things could be, though empirically speaking this might certainly prove to be the case . . . to back down from this vision would be to betray what one feels are the most precious powers and capacities of human beings; because however hard one tries, one simply cannot shake off the primitive conviction that *this is not how it is supposed to be*, however much we are conscious that this seeing the world in the light of Judgment Day, as Walter Benjamin might put it, is folly to the financiers and a stumbling block to stockbrokers; because there is something in this vision which calls to the depths of one's being and evokes a passionate assent there; because not to feel this would not to be oneself; because one is too much in love with this vision of humankind to back down, walk away, or take no for an answer.[38]

36. Theodore Adorno, *Minima Moralia: Reflections from Damaged Life*, 247, cited in Russell Jacoby, *The End of Utopia: Politics and Culture in an Age of Apathy* (New York: Basic, 1999), 181.

37. Jacoby, *End of Utopia*, 181.

38. Terry Eagleton, *Reason, Faith, and Revelation* (New Haven, CT/London: Yale University Press, 2009), 122–123 (emphasis original).

Most Marxist intellectuals eschew violence, not on moral grounds but because violent revolutions have always left a deeply ambiguous legacy. It is indeed arguable that few of the reforms in education, gender relationships and constitutional protections for minorities that most of us take for granted would have been possible without some degree of violence. In our fallen human world, it is the case that "Violence is sometimes needed for the voice of moderation to be heard."[39] Moreover, as Paulo Freire observed in his educational classic *Pedagogy of the Oppressed*, "Never in history has violence been initiated by the oppressed. How could they be the initiators, if they themselves are the result of violence?"[40] Freire also argued that attempts by revolutionary elites to liberate the oppressed without their reflective participation in the act of liberation was itself an act of violence against them. It was to "lead them into the populist pitfall and transform them into masses which can be manipulated." He cautioned, "When people are already dehumanized, due to the oppression they suffer, the process of their liberation must not employ the methods of dehumanization."[41]

Since all human action, save in the very short term, is fraught with uncertainty in that we don't know all the consequences of what we are doing, the church has generally frowned upon the use of violence in opposing aggression or despotism except as a final resort and then with very strict safeguards.[42] Violence very quickly snowballs and the means overwhelm the ends. As Hannah Arendt famously summed up: "The practice of violence, like all action, changes the world, but the most probable change is a more violent world."[43] However, non-violent resistance to wrongdoing is not to be confused with pacifism. Nor is coercion always violent. "Non-lethal coercion (as in a boycott, or peaceful march) that respects the integrity and personhood of the 'opponent' is not immoral or violent," writes Ron Sider. "By non-violence, I mean an activist confrontation with evil that respects the personhood even

39. The former Irish politician and philosopher Conor Cruise O'Brien, quoted in Hannah Arendt, "Reflections on Violence," *The New York Review of Books*, 11 July 2013.

40. Paulo Freire, *Pedagogy of the Oppressed* (1970), 30th anniversary ed. (New York/London: Continuum, 2003), 55.

41. Freire, *Pedagogy*, 65, 67.

42. One of the best modern expositions of this tradition is Oliver O'Donovan, *The Just War Revisited* (Cambridge: Cambridge University Press, 2003).

43. Arendt, "Reflections on Violence."

of the 'enemy' and therefore seeks both to end the oppression and reconcile the oppressor."[44]

The struggle against oppression often leads to "black-and-white" categorizations that fuel self-righteousness and resentment on the part of the victims and those who speak for them. This has been apparent in the *dalit* and *minjung* liberation theologies that have come to the fore in India and South Korea, respectively, since the 1970s. The *minjung* refers to the oppressed common people in traditional Korean society; *minjung* theology sees them as the "people of God" and gives their religious experience epistemic priority. However, "Some of the Korean Christian *minjung* who had been marginalized and oppressed by the ruling class in the 1970s later became an upper-middle class or members of the ruling political party of South Korea in the 1980s and 1990s. These people who used to be the *minjung* in the 1970s were being accused by others of being 'oppressors' as they became organized and acquired socio-political power."[45]

Dalit theology in India rightly reacts against the historical tendency in the Indian church to do theology "from above," in dialogue with the Hindu philosophical schools, and ignore the terrible oppression of the Hindu caste system (*dalits* are those who are excluded from this system and therefore treated as subhuman). In a sympathetic but also critical study of the *dalit* theologies that have emerged in India, Peniel Rajkumar observes that "*Dalit* theologians, more often than not, have exhibited a tendency to focus on the identity of the *dalits* only as 'victims of the caste-system.' They have maintained relative oblivion to the aspect of *dalits* as 'oppressors,' within the reality of intra-*dalit* hierarchy." He points out that the Indian caste system is so complex that in spite of deep differences there are some points of interrelatedness between the religious world of the caste communities and *dalit* communities: for instance, common religious festivals and places of pilgrimage. It is imperative, says Rajkumar, for *dalit* theology to move away from binary models of theologizing and acknowledge that "aspects of fluidity and hybridity constitute *dalit* identity, *dalit* religion and *dalit* existence." On this basis we can engage non-*dalits*, too, as co-partners in liberation. "This will pave the way for a praxis of mutual

---

44. Ron Sider, *Exploring the Limits of Non-Violence* (London: Hodder & Stoughton, 1988), 3.

45. Koo Dong Yun, "Pentecostalism from Below: *Minjung* Liberation and Asian Pentecostal Theology," in *The Spirit in the World: Emerging Pentecostal Theologies in Global Contexts*, ed. Veli-Matti Kärkkäinen (Grand Rapids, MI: Eerdmans, 2009), 97.

engagement, where both *dalits* and non-*dalits* can become partners in the struggle for justice and equality."[46]

The only way to mitigate the cruelties in social conflict, even if we can never eliminate them, argued Reinhold Niebuhr in an American context, is for those who suffer to refuse to adopt the same stance of moral superiority as those whom they oppose and not privilege the status of victimhood.[47] What he called the "spiritual discipline against resentment" in political struggle rests on the sense of sin and discriminates between the evils of a socio-political system and the individuals who are involved in it.

The Old Testament scholar Walter Brueggemann has delineated two "disciplines of resistance" – the liturgical and the ethical – in ancient Israel's attempt to live as an intentional, distinctive community in a world dominated by empires (Egypt, Assyria, Babylon).[48] For liturgical resistance, Brueggemann expounds Exodus 1–15 as the regular re-enactment of Israel's foundational story. As Israel participates in this drama, it imagines and construes a social world outside the hegemonic control of Pharaoh and other demi-gods. It affirms that "the *world constructed in liturgy* is more reliable and more credible than the world 'out there.'"[49]

This liturgy begins with the *public voicing of pain*: "The Israelites groaned in their slavery and cried out, and their cry for help because of their slavery went up to God. God heard their groaning and he remembered his covenant with Abraham, with Isaac and with Jacob" (Exod 2:23–24). This is the lament tradition which we have explored in previous chapters. The public voicing of pain defies the attempt of empire to silence its victims, and it is also a refusal to accept their status as slaves and their suffering in docility. The second element in the liturgy is a *critique that ridicules established power*. Brueggemann argues that the long recital of the plague narrative (Exod 7–11) is shot through with mockery whereby Yahweh "makes sport" with Pharaoh and erodes his authority. Taunting powerful kings and empires was a well-known literary genre among the prophets (e.g. Isa 14; Ezek 31; 32; Nahum) and the clearest New Testament example (weaving taunt into a funeral dirge) is the lament over Rome in Revelation 18.

---

46. Peniel Rajkumar, *Dalit Theology and Dalit Liberation: Problems, Paradigms and Possibilities* (Farnham: Ashgate, 2010), 170, 176.

47. See the chapter "Spiritual Disciplines against Resentment," in Lasch, *True and Only Heaven*, especially 376–378.

48. Walter Brueggemann, *Texts That Linger, Words That Explode: Listening to Prophetic Voices* (Minneapolis, MN: Fortress, 2000), 75–78.

49. Brueggemann, *Texts That Linger*, 76 (emphasis original).

Together with such liturgical resistance, Israel *developed rigorous disciplines* (the Torah) for the sake of an alternative community. After the Decalogue, the central commands which epitomized Israel's counter-practice were the keeping of the Sabbath and the "year of release" (Exod 21:1–11) which, in cancelling the debts of neighbours, enabled them to rejoin the economy as full and equal partners.[50] One could add to this the extension of the "year of release" to the Jubilee (Lev 25), when land ownership reverted to the original trustees. In Israel's understandings of land, work and celebration, it was called by Yahweh to practise a radical counter-economics. Brueggemann concludes: "This little community that begins in pain and ends in dancing, that stops its life for sabbath, that cancels debts for the sake of neighborliness, in the end this community has in its midst the force for life, and is the wave of the future."[51]

Hope as Waiting

In the course of this study, we have already encountered the blistering, passionate rhetoric of the Jewish polymath George Steiner, one of the towering literary and intellectual figures of his times. Here is Steiner again, in a moment of honest confession rarely found among Christian theologians or pastors:

> When I am confronted, via reports, pictures, personal notice, of the infliction of wanton pain on children and on animals, a despairing rage floods me. There are those who tear out the eyes of living children, who shoot children in the eyes, who beat animals across their eyes. These facts overwhelm me with desolate loathing. The hatred, the despair they unleash in me are far in excess of my mental and nervous resources . . . in the presence of the beaten, raped child, of the horse or mule flogged across its eyes, I am possessed, as by a midnight clarity, by the intuition of the Fall. Only some such happening, irretrievable to reason, can make intelligible, though always near to unbearable, the actualities of our history on this wasted earth. We are condemned to be our cruel, greedy, egotistical, mendacious selves. When it was, when it must have been meant to be *otherwise*. When the truth and

50. Brueggemann states that "this neighborly act of debt cancellation . . . is the taproot of all Jewish and Christian notions of forgiveness" (78). We should also note that the Jubilee was proclaimed, every fiftieth year, on the Day of Atonement. The restoration of capital followed the release from sin and guilt.

51. Brueggemann, 78.

> self-sacrificial compassion of exceptional men and women show so plainly what might have been. I have found myself wondering, fantasticating childishly, whether human history is not the passing nightmare of a sleeping god. Whether He will not wake from it so as to render unnecessary, once and for all, the scream of the child, the gagging of the beaten animal.[52]

Then Steiner concludes with the words, "But I am unable, even at the worst hours, to abdicate from the belief that the two validating wonders of mortal existence are love and the invention of the future tense. Their conjunction, if it will ever come to pass, is the Messianic."[53] Love and the future tense, combined in the messianic. Passionate longing, mingled with doubt whether the "sleeping god" will indeed wake up and set the world to rights.

Waiting for the Lord is a prominent motif in much of the Old Testament. "But as for me, I watch in hope for the LORD, I wait for God my Saviour; my God will hear me" (Mic 7:7). "I wait for the LORD, my whole being waits, and in his word I put my hope" (Ps 130:5). "Wait for the LORD; be strong and take heart and wait for the LORD" (Ps 27:14). "Yes, LORD, walking in the way of your laws, we wait for you; your name and renown are the desire of our hearts" (Isa 26:8).

Waiting in expectation, as opposed to mere idleness, is built into every form of human agency. The student puts her best effort into answering the examination paper and then awaits the results. The lover pours his heart into his letter to his beloved and waits eagerly for her response. The mother waits anxiously for the report of her sick daughter's MRI scan. Those who have worked tirelessly to oust a corrupt government wait for the election results. The defendant and her lawyers wait for the jury to deliver their verdict. Expectant waiting is both the climax of work and the recognition that we are temporal creatures and dependent on others. We saw in chapter 3 how Jesus's passivity and endurance – his passion – in the face of opposition was the climax of his mission. In putting himself in the hands of others, even asking their help ("I thirst"), he turned upside down the values of the modern Trinity: Autonomy, Activism, Achievement.

In our world of smartphones, machine intelligence and supercomputers, waiting can only be experienced as "frustration," a ubiquitous late-modern term, when the machine is too slow or the systems fail. But patience is an

---

52. George Steiner, *Errata: An Examined Life* (London: Weidenfeld & Nicolson, 1997), 168, 169.

53. Steiner, *Errata*, 170–171.

intrinsic aspect of being human. As embodied selves, we are limited in our activities by bodies that keep us from doing whatever we desire and whenever we desire it; as social selves, we are dependent on others for meeting our needs; and as temporal selves, we can only achieve our aims step by step, not all at once. "Patience is," David Harned writes, "simply the embrace of what we are. We are patients, whether we like it or not; we cannot escape our own nature. We come into the world as patients and we leave it as patients, but even in our days of greatest strength our condition is no different."[54] This need not imply passive acceptance of our present circumstances. But learning to live with unfulfilled desires, as well as unanswered questions, is a sign of maturity.

I mentioned earlier, in the course of exploring the suffering love of the Triune God, the way of "active" suffering: making what befalls us "our own." We know that often, perhaps in most cases, trauma can shatter and cripple people for the rest of their earthly lives. But there are also those who exhibit an extraordinary resilience in the face of horrendous suffering and grow in stature through hardship, illness and loss. Rev Martin Luther King, who would belong to this category, cited the biographer of the great eighteenth-century composer George Frederick Handel: "His health and his fortunes had reached the lowest ebb. His right side had become paralyzed, and his money was all gone. His creditors seized him and threatened him with imprisonment. For a long time he was tempted to give up the fight – but then he rebounded again to compose the greatest of his inspirations, the epic 'Messiah.'"[55] And here is Archbishop Desmond Tutu on the transformation of Nelson Mandela:

> People say, look at what he achieved in his years in government – what a waste those 27 years in prison were. I maintain his prison term was necessary because when he went to jail, he was angry. He was relatively young and had experienced a miscarriage of justice; he wasn't a statesperson, ready to be forgiving; he was commander-in-chief of the armed wing of the party, which was quite prepared to use violence. The time in jail was quite crucial. Of course, suffering embitters some people, but it ennobles others. Prison became a crucible that burned away the dross. People could never say to him: "You talk glibly of forgiveness. You haven't

---

54. David Baily Harned, *Patience: How We Wait upon the World* (Cambridge, MA: Cowley, 1997), 182.

55. Martin Luther King, *Strength to Love* (London: Fontana, 1969), 91.

> suffered. What do you know?" Twenty-seven years gave him the authority to say, let us try to forgive.[56]

There is a Persian fable about a very bitter man who hated everything young and beautiful and who was travelling in the desert. On the edge of an oasis he discovered a young palm tree growing up straight and lovely. In order to cripple the tree and destroy its beauty, the man fastened a heavy stone to the crown of the tree. No matter how hard the young tree tried, it could not shake off this stone. As it attempted, again and again without success, to get rid of this heavy burden, its roots thrust down deeper and deeper. They went down so deep that they soon reached the groundwater of the oasis. In spite of the burden of the rock, the palm grew to be tall and stately. When the traveller passed again, he looked to see what he thought he had destroyed. Instead, the queenly palm bowed to him and showed him the stone. "I have to thank you," it said; "you have made me strong."

Of course, the pain and the questions of grief never go away. If, like Steiner, I might be permitted a personal confession: I am convinced of the bodily resurrection of Christ for I can find no other plausible explanation for the origins of the remarkable movement we call the church. And the universality and unanimity of the church's claim, right from the outset – in contrast with the variety of "models" of how the death of Christ benefited humanity – adds to its credibility. However, at the same time, I struggle to make sense of how billions of people throughout history will one day be resurrected into the new creation that has dawned in Jesus's resurrection. Moreover, the biblical writers take it for granted that we shall recognize not only our loved ones but also all those who have gone before us. But how does such recognition happen, given that all our bodily organs have evolved to meet the conditions of biological life on this earth? How did Peter recognize Moses and Elijah on the Mount of Transfiguration? What aspects of our embodiment has Christ taken into the Godhead for eternity? Is it only our memories, characters and relationships that we take from this life into the next? Haunted by such questions, perhaps all that we who grieve need to be assured of is that what awaits is *more*, and not less, of all that we currently treasure of life. I have to recall constantly the words of Martin Luther: "We know no more about eternal life than children in the womb of their mother know about the world they are about to enter."[57]

---

56. Desmond Tutu, "Jail Embitters Some, But It Ennobled Him," *Guardian Weekly*, 13–19 December 2013, 5.

57. Cited in Allison, *Night Comes*, 149.

But we know, too, that Luther himself struggled with dark periods of depression and doubts concerning his preaching. In a letter penned on Reformation Day, 31 October 1943, Bonhoeffer wondered

> how it was [that] Luther's actions led to consequences which were the exact opposite of what he intended, and which overshadowed the last years of his life and work, so that he doubted the value of what he had achieved. He desired a real unity for both the Church and for Western Christendom, but the consequence was the ruin of both. He sought the "Freedom of the Christian Man," and the consequence was apathy and barbarism. He hoped to see the establishment of a genuine social order free from clerical privilege, and the outcome was the Peasants' Revolt, and soon afterwards the gradual dissolution of all real cohesion and order in society.[58]

Bonhoeffer continued, "Kierkegaard said more than a century ago that if Luther were alive then he would have said the exact opposite of what he said in the sixteenth century. I believe he was right."[59]

Hope in the Darkness

It has been well said that the opposite of faith is not doubt but the desire for certainty. In Isaiah 50:10, the despairing community in exile are challenged with these words:

> Who among you fears the LORD
> and obeys the word of his servant?
> Let the one who walks in the dark,
> who has no light,
> trust in the name of the LORD
> and rely on their God.

And in that great New Testament chapter about the heroes of faith, while the opening words are "Faith is confidence in what we hope for and assurance about what we do not see" (Heb 11:1), we almost immediately come to verse 8 which says of Abraham that he "obeyed and went, even though he did not know where he was going." Obedience and ignorance – many of us can identify

58. Dietrich Bonhoeffer, *Letters and Papers from Prison*, Eng. trans. (London: SCM, 1953; London: Collins, 1959), 31.

59. Bonhoeffer, *Letters and Papers*, 31–32.

with this, however contradictory it sounds when juxtaposed with the opening words! Faith is a matter of faithful obedience; and living with one's questions and without many certainties.

We find no description of the face of Jesus in the canonical Gospels.[60] His face is only mentioned in Luke's and Matthew's accounts of the transfiguration, where Matthew tells us that Jesus's face "shone like the sun" (Matt 17:2), clearly an anticipation of his future glory. Paul may well have this in mind when he tells the Corinthians that "God, who said, 'Let light shine out of darkness,' made his light shine in our hearts to give us the light of the knowledge of God's glory displayed in the face of Christ" (2 Cor 4:6). The light of creation in the first chapter of Genesis, and the light that enveloped Paul on the road to Damascus and led to his spiritual awakening, are anticipations of a new creation suffused with the glory of Christ.

Lest we settle into a complacent religious fundamentalism, we also need to heed Paul's warning that "we know in part and we prophesy in part, but when completeness comes, what is in part disappears . . . For now we see only a reflection as in a mirror; then we shall see face to face. Now I know in part; then I shall know fully, even as I am fully known" (1 Cor 13:9, 12). Recall that mirrors in Paul's day were not made of clear glass, but bronze. Our faces are also more than the sum of their particular features (such as ears, nose, lips or cheekbones). The face is "the subject revealing itself in the world of objects."[61] In face-to-face confrontation with someone I am encountering not a physical part of him or her, as I would if I were, say, a medical physician examining an eye or a knee. I encounter a person, a unique self-consciousness subject, who is revealed in the face while remaining hidden beyond it.

I have been told of a medieval Jewish belief that the reason why Moses and the ancient people of Israel were not given a glimpse of the face of God was not only because of the sin that blinds human vision, but because the face of God is so filled with anguish that the sight is unbearable. Whatever may be the truth of that (both the existence of that belief and its content), the image is deeply evocative. We have seen in this study – following the theological insights offered us by scholars such as Barth, Bonhoeffer, Kitamori, Fiddes, Moltmann and many others – that God is no stranger to suffering and mortality. While

60. Nor do we find any faces described anywhere in the Bible, although there are occasional references to long hair and beards. This may reflect the ancient Hebrew prohibition on images.

61. Roger Scruton, *The Face of God: The Gifford Lectures 2010* (London: Bloomsbury, 2012), 80. Scruton cites Emmanuel Levinas's description of the face as "in and of itself visitation and transcendence" and paraphrases this as "the face comes *into* our shared world from a place beyond it, while in some way *remaining* beyond it, always just out of reach" (74, emphasis original).

self-existent (depending on no other for his being), God has chosen not to be self-sufficient. He has chosen to be *God for us*; and that entails his choosing to be affected by us, to allow suffering and evil to befall him, while not being overcome by them. That also entails that God has a real future, in that his being is enriched by what his creation brings to him.

And here we return to that intriguing verse which we have partially explored: "my power is *made perfect* in weakness" (2 Cor 12:9). It seems that there is a future in which God's power, now not perfect or complete, will be made perfect or complete. And it happens through human weakness. Mystery of mysteries. We have seen in an earlier chapter that a real creation implies that God does not control or micromanage all that happens in the world and in our lives. While there is divine oversight and rule, there are also threats, setbacks and disruptions so that divine providence is not instantiated everywhere and all the time. In fact, the Lord bids his church to pray "Your will be done, on earth as it is in heaven" because his will is *not* now done on earth. And the consummation of God in the final reign of Christ over the universe will also be the perfection of God's vulnerable power.

Paul Fiddes speaks of the "perfect incompleteness of God."[62] In desiring to bring many sons and daughters to glory (Heb 2:10) God too is glorified. Traditionally, this has been understood as God's glory as creator and redeemer being revealed and finally acknowledged by his creation. While this is true, Fiddes boldly proposes that God also *receives* glory from his perfected creation. It is the glory that arises from the fulfilment of his desire for his creation. But while God, unlike us, has the perfect and sure hope that in the end he will unify all things with himself, the content of that event depends upon the response of his creatures. And this raises the possibility that the ultimate triumph of God may also include an element of loss, not for us but for God:

> While God will finally reconcile all things, there is an openness about the nature of the world that will be reconciled. Doubtless, created beings will feel nothing lacking in their vision of God; they will be satisfied by the glory of their destination, deeper into God. But God may feel the tragedy that the world has not fulfilled all the divine aims for it, or has failed to realise them in

62. "Indeed, God – to remain God – cannot be degraded through change but can only move from one degree of glory to another. Here we may distinguish between divine perfection and divine completion: while never less than perfectly related to everything God has made, God in sovereign freedom may choose to be completed through relating to it. God will be perfect in relation to amoral organic life at the amoeba stage, in a different way from being perfect in relation to persons in need of forgiveness." Paul Fiddes, *Participating in God: A Pastoral Doctrine of the Trinity* (London: Darton, Longman & Todd, 2000), 210–211.

> the way that would bring about the maximum beauty and value. Such a possibility does not eternalise evil in God, because the reality which will be in existence will be wholly good, and the past marked by evil will have been transformed; yet God may still feel pain over the absence of some good that might have been achieved. In humility, God is prepared to know that there is a lack within the final reconciliation of the universe, where we are sublimely unaware of anything missing at all. This is a limited risk, but a real one.[63]

We have seen how familiarity with the Gospel narratives, and an unfortunate theological tendency to substitute doctrine for narrative, often blunts our sensibilities and brings us to a premature closure in proclaiming the message of Easter. Because we know "how the story ends," we do not strive to enter, as far as that is imaginatively possible, into the experience of the first disciples of Jesus: their sense of shock, betrayal, disillusionment and even anger at a God who was either helpless in the face of rampant evil or had deliberately deceived them. It is why we need to *linger* in Easter Saturday, the "in-between" day, when all hope was shattered, God silenced, and evil seemingly triumphant.[64] Unless we do so, we shall fail to grasp the sheer wonder of Easter, just as we cannot appreciate the dawn without experiencing the sheer darkness of the night. Easter Sunday cannot be "played off" against Good Friday, as if God was absent in one and present in the other. Each illuminates the other. The risen Christ is still the Christ who was tortured, crucified and entombed. It is he, and no other, who has been raised to life.

Humanity lives today in Easter Saturday. Countless people experience life as godless or God-forsaken, history as simply "one damned thing after another" (in a memorable phrase often attributed to Henry Ford). The church, that section of humanity which has glimpsed the dawn in Easter Sunday while sharing the agony of Easter Saturday in fellowship with the rest of humanity, seeks to witness to that dawn through its common life and practices in the world. The resurrection and exaltation of Christ do not mean that his story has now reached closure. Rather, the resurrection breaks open new possibilities, new horizons, which involve us who are now united with Christ through the Holy Spirit who groans, empowers and sanctifies. The story continues.

---

63. Fiddes, *Participating in God*, 141–142.

64. This is the burden of the late Alan Lewis's book which has often been referred to above. It could be read as a prolonged meditation on the words of the Nicene Creed that say that Christ "was crucified, died, *and was buried*," underlining the finality of his death, before proceeding to "On the third day . . . "

6

Epilogue

Blind unbelief is sure to err," wrote the English hymn-writer William Cowper (1731–1800). Blind belief also errs, and its errors have had dreadful consequences, from the torture of heretics to acts of mass terror. Those who claim to be religious traditionalists are often ignorant about their traditions and tend to ignore or edit those parts which embrace ambiguity, nuance, irony, paradox and even contradiction. Doctrinal reformations and moral revolutions in the church remind us that Christians have often got things wrong as well as right. Such a historical perspective keeps us humble, always eager to learn from others as well as to share with others beliefs that have withstood the tests of time and place.

While speaking, a few years ago, at an American university, I was asked a question about global warming. I said that climate change, as a result of global warming, was not only a fact but now irreversible, and that severe climatic events lay ahead. A Christian student stood up and angrily remonstrated: "How can you believe that?" he asked; "Where is your Christian hope?" I replied that I saw nothing in the Bible to lead me to believe that hope in the eschatological reign of God in the new creation should entail that humanity and the earth will be spared either natural or man-made catastrophes. And Christians in the rich world, who have contributed to global warming, whether through selfish lifestyles, bad teaching, complicity in ruthless corporate greed or sheer ignorance, have no right to proclaim "hope" without public acts of repentance. Moreover, our penultimate hopes depend on us as much as on God's actions, while our ultimate hope is based not in our ourselves but on the promises of God.

I have argued in this brief study that lament and joy, faith and doubt, clarity and ambiguity, belong together in Christian living. Indeed, faith is about faithfulness in action rather than knowing all the "right doctrines." Mystery and paradox are at the heart of the gospel, and should be central to any Christian proclamation. It is only through obedience to Christ that we grow in our conviction that he *is* the Christ. It is by living in the darkness, and choosing (like God) to participate in the darkness of others, that we catch glimpses of new creation.

We care for God's creation, human and non-human, because our love for God entails loving all that God loves.[1] Towards the end of P. D. James's novel *The Private Patient*, a character (not a Christian) pensively shares her thoughts on life: "The world is a beautiful and terrible place. Deeds of horror are committed every minute and in the end those we love die. If the screams of all earth's living creatures were one scream of pain, surely it would shake the stars. But we have love. It may seem a fragile defence against the horrors of the world but we must hold fast and believe in it, for it is all that we have."[2]

The Italian chemist Primo Levi survived Auschwitz and wrote several reflective accounts of that experience. His book *If This Is a Man* is an extraordinary account of his life as a slave on rations that were not sufficient to sustain life. He was saved from death by Lorenzo, a non-Jewish Italian who was working for the Germans as a civilian on an industrial project using prisoners as labourers. Levi tells us what Lorenzo meant to him:

> In concrete terms it amounts to little: an Italian civilian worker brought me a piece of bread and the remainder of his ration every day for six months; he gave me a vest of his, full of patches; he wrote a postcard on my behalf to Italy and brought me the reply. For all this he neither asked nor accepted any reward, because he was good and simple and did not think that one did good for a reward . . .
>
> I believe that it was really due to Lorenzo that I am alive today; and not so much for his material aid, as for his having constantly reminded me by his presence, by his natural and plain manner of being good, that there still existed a just world outside our own,

---

1. Here I part company with those who expend a lot of ink arguing over the proper translation of texts like 2 Pet 3:10 which have normally been taken to mean the final destruction of the earth. While I agree that "disclosed" is a better translation than "dissolved/destroyed" in this verse, I fail to see what great difference it makes to our ethic of creation care. After all, we care daily for our bodies, our houses and much else that we know is perishing. And, furthermore, should we necessarily share the very limited cosmology of the biblical writers so that we cannot envisage a future home on another planet in our gigantic visible universe, let alone invisible realms?

2. P. D. James, *The Private Patient* (London: Penguin, 2009), 497–498.

> something and someone still pure and whole, not corrupt, not savage, extraneous to hatred and terror; something difficult to define, a remote possibility of good, but for which it was worth surviving.[3]

I am sure there are men and women like Lorenzo among the refugees and prisoners in Syria, Gaza, Iraq and elsewhere, who have not lost their essential humanity. We shall, no doubt, read their stories one day. But, in the meantime, it is hard not to feel sickened at the unending savagery paraded before our eyes on TV screens, newspapers and on the Internet. But is apathy, the deadening of emotion, the cynical attitude of "let them all kill themselves out there," not also obnoxious? It is understandable when the indifference is born of fear for one's life; but usually it stems from the fear of having to change our views if we do start asking questions about what lies behind these stories of violent conflict and recognize the complicity of our own nations.

Raising such uncomfortable questions, showing mercy and compassion to strangers, are the Christlike acts to which we are all called, whether as Christians or otherwise. "In concrete terms they may amount to little," as Levi would put it. There is nothing "ordinary" in what a Christian or anyone with a passionate faith does. Working in an office, living in an obscure village, we may feel that what we are doing is ordinary, mere routine. We do not seem to be having an impact on what we think are the great epoch-making events of human history. But all the great movements in history had "small beginnings." Just recall an Augustinian monk nailing his ninety-five theses to a church door in the German town of Wittenberg in 1517; a black seamstress, Rosa Parks, boarding a bus in Montgomery, Alabama, and defying the law on racial segregation; or a young English lawyer, Peter Benenson, writing a newspaper article in 1961 suggesting that people should come together to voice their disgust at the imprisonment of political or religious dissidents – and so giving birth to Amnesty International.[4] Even as I write, a Swedish teenager, Greta Thunberg, has unleashed a worldwide movement among students demanding that their governments translate talk on reducing carbon emissions into concrete action.

---

3. Primo Levi, *If This Is a Man* (1958; London: Everyman, 2000), 145.

4. "Open your newspaper any day of the week and you will find a report from somewhere in the world of someone being imprisoned, tortured or executed because his opinions or religion are unacceptable to his government . . . The newspaper reader feels a sickening sense of impotence. Yet if these feelings of disgust could be united into common action, something effective could be done." Peter Benenson, "The Forgotten Prisoners," *The Observer*, 28 May 1961.

And what can Christians say to those who wield power in our nations and to all who confront others over ideology, race or territory? That the crucified and risen Christ exposes the hollowness of all talk of "national security" based on creating victims; that aggression, retaliation, self-assertion and self-protection only unleash new demons; that there is a protective and enabling strength that is discovered through vulnerability, trust and collective repentance; and that, as in the case of individuals, national welfare is better served by hazarding identity and taking risks in the service of transnational goods.

I conclude this meditation with the exhortation of a British theologian, Timothy Gorringe, to Christians

> to tell the [gospel] story, trust in God, pray in the darkness, act for justice as the prophets commanded, and cheerfully wait to see what happens. What transpires will be the redemption of modernity, or postmodernity, as what happened from the fifth century on was the redemption of what we call the "dark ages." It depends on our cultural imagination, on our creativity, on the search for the best which both has been and will be thought and known. But it depends even more on hope in the God who calls the dead to life.[5]

5. Timothy J. Gorringe, *Furthering Humanity: A Theology of Culture* (Aldershot: Ashgate, 2004), 266.

Bibliography

Abraham, William J. *Among the Ashes: On Death, Grief, and Hope*. Grand Rapids, MI: Eerdmans, 2017.

Alexander, Denis R. *Is There Purpose in Biology? The Cost of Existence and the God of Love*. Oxford: Lion Hudson, 2018.

———. *Rebuilding the Matrix: Science and Faith in the 21st Century*. Oxford: Lion, 2001.

Allen, Leslie C. *A Liturgy of Grief: A Pastoral Commentary on Lamentations*. Grand Rapids, MI: Baker Academic, 2011.

Allison, Jr., Dale C. *Night Comes: Death, Imagination, and the Last Things*. Grand Rapids, MI: Eerdmans, 2016.

Anselm of Canterbury. Edited and translated by Jasper Hopkins and Herbert Richardson. 4 vols. New York: Edwin Mellen Press, 1976.

Arendt, Hannah. "Reflections on Violence." *The New York Review of Books*. 11 July 2013. http://www.nybooks.com/articles/archives/2013/jul/11/hannah-arendt-reflections-violence/.

Asad, Talal. "Thinking about Agency and Pain." In *Formations of the Secular: Christianity, Islam, Modernity*. Stanford, CA: Stanford University Press, 2003.

Atkinson, David. *The Message of Job*. Leicester: Inter-Varsity Press, 1991.

Barth, Karl. *Church Dogmatics*, IV/1. Translated and edited by G. W. Bromiley and T. F. Torrance. Edinburgh: T&T Clark, 1936–77.

Bauckham, Richard. "The Incarnation and the Cosmic Christ." In *Incarnation: On the Scope and Depth of Christology*, edited by Niels Henrik Gregersen, 55–58. Minneapolis, MN: Fortress, 2015.

———. *The Theology of Jürgen Moltmann*. Edinburgh: T&T Clark, 1995.

Beckwith, Francis J. "Dignity Never Been Photographed: Scientific Materialism, Enlightenment Liberalism, and Steven Pinker." *Ethics & Medicine* 26, no. 2 (Summer 2010): 93–100.

Begbie, Jeremy. *Resounding Truth: Christian Wisdom in the World of Music*. London: SPCK, 2007.

Benenson, Peter. "The Forgotten Prisoners." *The Observer*, 28 May 1961.

Bimson, John J. "Reconsidering a 'Cosmic Fall.'" *Science and Christian Belief* 18, no. 1 (April 2006): 63–81.

Blocher, Henri. *Evil and the Cross*. Translated by David G. Preston. Downers Grove, IL: InterVarsity Press, 1994.

Bonhoeffer, Dietrich. *Letters and Papers from Prison*. English translation. London: SCM, 1953; London: Collins, 1959.

Brown, Peter. *Augustine of Hippo: A Biography*. Berkeley, CA: University of California Press, 1967.

———. *Poverty and Leadership in the Later Roman Empire: The Menahem Stern Jerusalem Lectures*. Hanover, NH: University Press of New England, 2002.

Brueggemann, Walter. *The Message of the Psalms*. Minneapolis, MN: Augsburg Press, 1984.

———. *The Prophetic Imagination*. 2nd ed. Minneapolis, MN: Fortress, 2001.

———. *Texts That Linger, Words That Explode: Listening to Prophetic Voices*. Minneapolis, MN: Fortress, 2000.

Burdett, Michael. "The Changing Face of Evolutionary Theory?" BioLogos. 2 March 2015. http://biologos.org/blogs/archive/the-changing-face-of-evolutionary-theory.

Calvin, John. *Institutes of the Christian Religion*. Edited by John T. McNeill. 2 vols. Philadelphia: Westminster, 1960.

Cardenal, Ernesto. *Marilyn Monroe and Other Poems*. Translated by Robert Pring-Mill. London: Search Press, 1975.

Centers for Disease Control and Prevention. "1918 Pandemic (H1N1 Virus)." https://www.cdc.gov/flu/pandemic-resources/1918-pandemic-h1n1.html.

Charry, Ellen T. "The Uniqueness of Christ in Relation to Jewish People: The Eternal Crusade." In *Christ the One and Only*, edited by Sung Wook Chung, 136–161. Milton Keynes: Paternoster; Grand Rapids, MI: Baker, 2005.

Chomsky, Noam. *Imperial Ambitions: Conversations on the Post-9/11 World*. New York: Metropolitan Books, 2005.

Ciano, Rachel. "Lament Psalms in the Church." In *Finding Lost Words: The Church's Right to Lament*, edited by G. Geoffrey Harper and Kit Barker, 9–23. Eugene, OR: Wipf & Stock, 2017.

"The Council of Florence (A.D. 1438–1445) from Cantate Domino – Papal Bull of Pope Eugene IV." Catholicism.org. 16 March 2005. https://catholicism.org/cantate-domino.html.

Dawkins, Richard. *The Blind Watchmaker*. New York: W. W. Norton, 1986.

———. *River Out of Eden: A Darwinian View*. New York: Basic, 1995.

de Botton, Alain. *Status Anxiety*. First published 2004. Harmondsworth: Penguin, 2005.

de Unamuno, Miguel. "The Tragic Sense of Life." In *Men and Nations*. Translated by A. Kerrigan. London: Routledge and Kegan Paul, 1972.

de Waal, Esther. *Lost in Wonder: Rediscovering the Spiritual Art of Attentiveness*. Toronto: Novalis, 2003.

Dembski, William. *The End of Christianity: Finding a Good God in an Evil World*. Nashville: B&H, 2009.

Eagleton, Terry. *Reason, Faith, and Revelation*. New Haven, CT: Yale University Press, 2009.

Edwards, Denis. "The Redemption of Animals in an Incarnational Theology." In *Creaturely Theology: On God, Humans, and Other Animals*, edited by Celia Deane-Drummond and David Clough, 81–99. London: SCM, 2009.

Eiesland, Nancy. *The Disabled God: Towards a Liberatory Theology of Disability*. Nashville: Abingdon Press, 1994.

Eliot, T. S. *Murder in the Cathedral*. New York: Harcourt Brace Jovanovich, 1935.

Ellington, Scott A. *Risking Truth: Reshaping the World through Prayers of Lament*. Eugene, OR: Pickwick, 2008.

Falk, Darrel R. "Theological Challenges Faced by Darwin." In *Darwin, Creation and the Fall: Theological Challenges*, edited by R. J. Berry and T. A. Noble, 75–85. Nottingham: Apollos, 2009.

Fergusson, David. *The Providence of God: A Polyphonic Approach*. Cambridge: Cambridge University Press, 2018.

Fern, Richard L. *Nature, God and Humanity: Envisioning an Ethics of Nature*. Cambridge: Cambridge University Press, 2002.

Fiddes, Paul. *The Creative Suffering of God*. Oxford: Clarendon Press, 1988.

———. *Participating in God: A Pastoral Doctrine of the Trinity*. London: Darton, Longman & Todd, 2000.

Flannery, Tim. "The Amazing Inner Lives of Animals." *New York Review of Books*. 8 October 2015, 20.

Fraser, Giles. *Redeeming Nietzsche: On the Piety of Unbelief*. London; New York: Routledge, 2002.

Freire, Paulo. *Pedagogy of the Oppressed*. 30th anniversary ed. New York; London: Continuum, 2003.

Fretheim, Terence E. *The Suffering of God: An Old Testament Perspective*. Philadelphia: Fortress, 1984.

Fung, Raymond. "Evangelism Today." In *Living Theology in Asia*, edited by John England. London: SCM, 1981.

Garvey, Jon. *God's Good Earth: The Case for an Unfallen Creation*. Eugene, OR: Cascade, 2019.

Gawande, Atul. *Being Mortal: Illness, Medicine, and What Matters in the End*. London: Profile, 2014.

Gill, Malcolm J. "Praying Lament." In *Finding Lost Words: The Church's Right to Lament*, edited by G. Geoffrey Harper and Kit Barker, 223–236. Eugene, OR: Wipf & Stock, 2017.

Gorringe, Timothy J. *Furthering Humanity: A Theology of Culture*. Aldershot: Ashgate, 2004.

Gregersen, Niels Henrik. "Deep Incarnation: Why Evolutionary Continuity Matters in Christology." *Toronto Journal of Theology* 26, no. 2 (2010): 173–188.

———. "The Extended Body of Christ: Three Dimensions of Deep Incarnation." In *Incarnation: On the Scope and Depth of Christology*, edited by Niels Henrik Gregersen, 225–254. Minneapolis, MN: Fortress, 2015.

Gutiérrez, Gustavo. *On Job: God-Talk and the Suffering of the Innocent*. English translation. Maryknoll, NY: Orbis, 1987.

Harned, David Baily. *Patience: How We Wait upon the World*. Cambridge, MA: Cowley, 1997.

Harries, Richard. *Art and the Beauty of God*. New York; London: Continuum, 1993.

Hays, Richard B. *The Moral Vision of the New Testament: A Contemporary Introduction to New Testament Ethics.* New York: HarperCollins, 1996.

Hengel, Martin. *The Crucifixion of the Son of God.* London: SCM, 1986.

Herman, Bruce. "Wounds and Beauty." In *The Beauty of God: Theology and the Arts,* edited by Daniel J. Treier, Mark Husbands and Roger Lundin, 110–120. Downers Grove, IL: IVP Academic, 2007.

Jacoby, Russell. *The End of Utopia: Politics and Culture in an Age of Apathy.* New York: Basic, 1999.

James, P. D. *The Private Patient.* London: Penguin, 2009.

Jüngel, Eberhard. *God As the Mystery of the World.* Translated by D. L. Guder. Edinburgh: T&T Clark, 1983.

Kagan, Jerome. *Three Seductive Ideas.* Cambridge, MA: Harvard University Press, 1998.

Katongole, Emmanuel. *Born from Lament: The Theology and Politics of Hope in Africa.* Grand Rapids, MI: Eerdmans, 2017.

Kelly, J. N. D. *Early Christian Doctrines.* 5th ed. London: A&C Black, 1977. First published 1958.

Khilnani, Sunil. "Nehru's Faith." 34th Jawaharlal Nehru Memorial Lecture, Delhi. 13 November 2002.

Kierkegaard, Søren. *Journals of Soren Kierkegaard: A Selection.* Edited and translated by A. Dru. London: Fontana, 1958.

King, Martin Luther. *Strength to Love.* London: Fontana, 1969.

Kingsley, Charles. "The Natural Theology of the Future." 1871. The Literature Network. http://www.online-literature.com/charles-kingsley/scientific/7/.

Kitamori, Kazoh. *Theology of the Pain of God.* Translated by M. E. Bratcher. London: SCM, 1966.

Lasch, Christopher. *The True and Only Heaven: Progress and Its Critics.* New York: W. W. Norton, 1991.

Lee, Nancy C. *Lyrics of Lament: From Tragedy to Transformation.* Minneapolis, MN: Fortress, 2010.

Levi, Primo. *If This Is a Man.* First published 1958. London: Everyman, 2000.

Lewis, Alan E. *Between Cross and Resurrection: A Theology of Holy Saturday.* Grand Rapids, MI: Eerdmans, 2001.

Lewis, C. S. *A Grief Observed.* London: Faber & Faber, 1961.

———. *The Problem of Pain.* First published 1940. London: Collins, 1957.

Lewontin, Richard. "It's Even Less in Your Genes." *New York Review of Books.* 26 May 2011, 23.

Louth, Andrew. *Denys the Areopagite.* London: Geoffrey Chapman, 1989.

McCabe, Herbert. "Life after Death." In *The McCabe Reader*, edited by Brian Davies and Paul Kucharski, 353–358. London: Bloomsbury T&T Clark, 2016.

McConville, J. Gordon, and Stephen N. Williams. *Joshua.* Grand Rapids, MI: Eerdmans, 2010.

McGrath, Alister. *The Twilight of Atheism: The Rise and Fall of Disbelief in the Modern World.* London: Rider, 2004.

Meilaender, Gilbert. *Neither Beast nor God.* New York: Encounter Books, 2009.

———. *Should We Live Forever? The Ethical Ambiguities of Aging.* Grand Rapids, MI: Eerdmans, 2013.

Michaels, J. Ramsay. "Redemption of the Body: The Riddle of Romans 8:19–22." In *Romans and the People of God*, edited by Sven K. Soderlund and N. T. Wright, 92–115. Grand Rapids, MI: Eerdmans, 2000.

Moltmann, Jürgen. *The Coming of God: Christian Eschatology.* Minneapolis, MN: Fortress, 1996.

———. *The Crucified God.* London: SCM, 1974.

———. *God in Creation.* Minneapolis, MN: Fortress, 1993.

———. *The Way of Jesus Christ: Christology in Messianic Dimension.* San Francisco: Harper, 1990.

Mooney, Bel. *Devout Sceptics: Conversations on Faith and Doubt.* London: Hodder & Stoughton, 2004.

Mugambi, Jesse. *From Liberation to Reconstruction: African Christian Theology after the Cold War.* Nairobi: East African Educational Publishers, 1995.

Newbigin, Lesslie. *The Open Secret.* London: SPCK, 1978.

Nouwen, Henri. "Adam's Story: The Peace That Is Not of This World." *Weavings*, Mar–Apr 1988.

Nowak, Martin A. "Five Rules for the Evolution of Cooperation." In *Evolution, Games and God: The Principle of Cooperation*, edited by Martin A. Nowak and Sarah Coakley, 99–114. Cambridge, MA: Harvard University Press, 2013.

O'Donovan, Oliver. *The Desire of the Nations: Rediscovering the Roots of Political Theology.* Cambridge: Cambridge University Press, 1996.

———. *The Just War Revisited.* Cambridge: Cambridge University Press, 2003.

Osborn, Ronald E. *Death before the Fall: Biblical Literalism and the Problem of Animal Suffering.* Downers Grove, IL: InterVarsity Press, 2014.

Parratt, John. *Reinventing Christianity: African Theology Today.* Grand Rapids, MI: Eerdmans; Trenton, NJ: Africa World Press, 1995.

Penchansky, David. *The Betrayal of God: Ideological Conflict in Job.* Louisville, KY: Westminster John Knox Press, 1990.

Plantinga, Theodore. *Learning to Live with Evil.* Grand Rapids, MI: Eerdmans, 1982.

Polkinghorne, John. *The Faith of a Physicist: Reflections of a Bottom-Up Thinker, The Gifford Lectures, 1993–4.* Minneapolis, MN: Fortress, 1996.

———. *Science and Providence.* London: SPCK, 1989.

Ponting, Clive. *Churchill.* London: Sinclair-Stevenson, 1994.

Pope Benedict XVI. *Great Christian Thinkers: From the Early Church through the Middle Ages.* London: SPCK, 2011.

Pope Francis. *Evangelii Gaudium.* London: Catholic Truth Society, 2013.

Rahner, Karl. *Encounters with Silence.* Westminster, MD: Newman Press, 1965.

Rajkumar, Peniel. *Dalit Theology and Dalit Liberation: Problems, Paradigms and Possibilities.* Farnham: Ashgate, 2010.

Ramachandra, Vinoth. *Gods That Fail: Modern Idolatry and Christian Mission.* 2nd ed. Eugene, OR: Wipf & Stock, 2016. First published 1996.

———. *Subverting Global Myths: Theology and the Public Issues Shaping Our World.* London: SPCK; Downers Grove, IL: IVP Academic, 2008.

Rolston III, Holmes. *Science and Religion: A Critical Survey.* First published 1987. Reprinted. Philadelphia; London: Templeton Foundation, 2006.

Rupp, Gordon. *The Righteousness of God.* London: Hodder & Stoughton, 1953.

Russell, Richard J. *Cosmology from Alpha to Omega.* Minneapolis, MN: Fortress, 2008.

Sacks, Jonathan. *The Dignity of Difference.* London; New York: Continuum, 2002.

———. *Future Tense: A Vision for Jews and Judaism in the Global Culture.* London: Hodder & Stoughton, 2009.

Scruton, Roger. *The Face of God: The Gifford Lectures 2010.* London: Bloomsbury, 2012.

Sider, Ron. *Exploring the Limits of Non-Violence.* London: Hodder & Stoughton, 1988.

Sittser, Jerry. *A Grace Disguised.* Grand Rapids, MI: Zondervan, 2004.

Smith, David. *Stumbling towards Zion.* Carlisle: Langham Global Library, 2019.

Sobrino, Jon. *Where Is God? Earthquake, Terrorism, Barbarity, and Hope.* Translated by Margaret Wilde. Maryknoll, NY: Orbis, 2004.

Soskice, Janet Martin. *Metaphor and Religious Language.* First published 1985. Oxford: Clarendon, 1987.

Southgate, Christopher. *The Groaning of Creation: God, Evolution, and the Problem of Evil.* Louisville, KY: Westminster John Knox Press, 2008.

Spufford, Margaret. *Celebration.* Glasgow: Collins, 1989.

St Athanasius. *On the Incarnation.* Edited and translated by Robert W. Thomson. Oxford: Clarendon Press, 1971.

Stanley, Brian. *Christianity in the Twentieth Century: A World History.* Princeton, NJ: Princeton University Press, 2018.

Steiner, George. *Errata: An Examined Life.* London: Weidenfeld & Nicolson, 1997.

Taylor, John V. *The Christlike God.* London: SCM, 1992.

Tutu, Desmond. "Jail Embitters Some, but It Ennobled Him." *Guardian Weekly.* 13–19 December 2013, 5.

United Nations Human Development Report 2005. New York: UNDP, 2005.

Vanstone, W. H. *The Stature of Waiting.* First published 1982. London: Darton, Longman & Todd, 2004.

Wallace, Alfred Russel. *Darwinism.* First published 1889. 2nd ed. London: Macmillan and Co., 1897. https://people.wku.edu/charles.smith/wallace/arwbooks/xx_Wallace_Darwinism1897.pdf.

Weems, Ann. *Psalms of Lament.* Louisville, KY: Westminster John Knox Press, 1995.

Westermann, Claus. "The Role of the Lament in the Theology of the Old Testament." *Interpretation* 28 (Jan 1974): 20–38.

———. "The Two Faces of Job." In *Job and the Silence of God*, edited by Christian Duquoc and Casiano Floristan, 15–22. Concilium 169. New York: Seabury, 1983.

Williams, Clifford. *Existential Reasons for Belief in God: A Defense of Desires and Emotions for Faith*. Downers Grove, IL: IVP Academic, 2011.

Williams, Rowan. *Being Human: Bodies, Minds, Persons*. London: SPCK, 2018.

Wolterstorff, Nicholas. "Calvin and the Wounds of God." *Reformed Journal* 37, no. 6 (June 1987): 14–22.

———. "If God Is Good and Sovereign, Why Lament?" In Nicholas Wolterstorff, *Hearing the Call: Liturgy, Justice, Church and World*. Edited by Mark R. Gornik and Gregory Thompson. Grand Rapids, MI: Eerdmans, 2011.

———. *Lament for a Son*. Grand Rapids, MI: Eerdmans, 1987.

Wong, Gordon. *God, Why?: Habakkuk's Struggle with Faith in a World out of Control*. Singapore: Armour, 2007.

Wright, N. T. *Jesus and the Victory of God*. London: SPCK, 1996.

Yancey, Philip. *The Question That Never Goes Away*. Grand Rapids, MI: Zondervan, 2013.

Young, Frances. "Wisdom in Weakness." *Theology* 114, no. 3 (May/June 2011): 181–188.

Yun, Koo Dong. "Pentecostalism from Below: *Minjung* Liberation and Asian Pentecostal Theology." In *The Spirit in the World: Emerging Pentecostal Theologies in Global Contexts*, edited by Veli-Matti Kärkkäinen, 89–114. Grand Rapids, MI: Eerdmans, 2009.

Langham Literature and its imprints are a ministry of Langham Partnership.

Langham Partnership is a global fellowship working in pursuit of the vision God entrusted to its founder John Stott –

> ***to facilitate the growth of the church in maturity and Christ-likeness through raising the standards of biblical preaching and teaching.***

Our vision is to see churches in the Majority World equipped for mission and growing to maturity in Christ through the ministry of pastors and leaders who believe, teach and live by the word of God.

Our mission is to strengthen the ministry of the word of God through:

- nurturing national movements for biblical preaching
- fostering the creation and distribution of evangelical literature
- enhancing evangelical theological education

especially in countries where churches are under-resourced.

Our ministry

Langham Preaching partners with national leaders to nurture indigenous biblical preaching movements for pastors and lay preachers all around the world. With the support of a team of trainers from many countries, a multi-level programme of seminars provides practical training, and is followed by a programme for training local facilitators. Local preachers' groups and national and regional networks ensure continuity and ongoing development, seeking to build vigorous movements committed to Bible exposition.

Langham Literature provides Majority World preachers, scholars and seminary libraries with evangelical books and electronic resources through publishing and distribution, grants and discounts. The programme also fosters the creation of indigenous evangelical books in many languages, through writer's grants, strengthening local evangelical publishing houses, and investment in major regional literature projects, such as one volume Bible commentaries like *The Africa Bible Commentary* and *The South Asia Bible Commentary*.

Langham Scholars provides financial support for evangelical doctoral students from the Majority World so that, when they return home, they may train pastors and other Christian leaders with sound, biblical and theological teaching. This programme equips those who equip others. Langham Scholars also works in partnership with Majority World seminaries in strengthening evangelical theological education. A growing number of Langham Scholars study in high quality doctoral programmes in the Majority World itself. As well as teaching the next generation of pastors, graduated Langham Scholars exercise significant influence through their writing and leadership.

To learn more about Langham Partnership and the work we do visit **langham.org**

www.ingramcontent.com/pod-product-compliance
Lightning Source LLC
LaVergne TN
LVHW010107170826
845678LV00012B/2283

9781783688579